THE LINCOLN FUNERAL

THE LINCOLN FUNERAL

AN ILLUSTRATED HISTORY

MICHAEL LEAVY

WESTHOLME
Yardley

Acknowledgments
I am grateful for the patience and advice provided by Westholme publisher Bruce H. Franklin, editor Ron Silverman, friends Richard Panke and Michael Isabella, and daughter Rebecca Leavy.

Facing title page: Crowds surge around Lincoln's hearse in Philadelphia. (*Library of Congress*)

Westholme Publishing, LLC
904 Edgewood Road
Yardley, Pennsylvania 19067
Visit our Web site at www.westholmepublishing.com

First Printing June 2015
10 9 8 7 6 5 4 3 2 1
ISBN: 978-1-59416-227-5
Also available as an eBook.

Printed in the United States of America

For my daughter Rachel Leavy

CONTENTS

INTRODUCTION

It was America's first glamour war. Owing principally to photography, the horror and the heroics, the mundane of daily soldier life and the shock of cities reduced to smoldering rubble drew gasps from families seeing these images through stereo viewers or on cartes de visite. Out of the fiery turbulence of the Civil War strode gods. Foremost were Abraham Lincoln, then Ulysses S. Grant and Robert E. Lee, Jefferson Davis, Thomas "Stonewall" Jackson, and a host of lesser gods. And they were gods that got Americans killed by the hundreds of thousands.

America was a nation fighting to survive while still unsure of its real identity. Although steadfast to its concept of individual liberty, it still emulated Europe in everything from the proper way to hold a teacup to the best way to forge steel. But at the end of the war, a strange and refreshing social evolution had occurred. The nation's confidence had deepened from having survived a terrible war and the loss of its leader. An American identity would begin to emerge with distinct approaches to architecture, music, art, industry, and education. Although it would take generations for the war's wounds to heal, the future was hopeful and filled with promise.

The world had come to doubt, because of the catastrophe of the Civil War, the survivability of America and its great experiment in freedom. But the battered, bloodied nation believed it had in some ways been reborn. The brave experiment would continue. These sentiments were not expressed in chest-pounding victory cries but in the shedding of tears as mourners followed the casket of the assassinated Lincoln like the ancients followed a beloved pharaoh to his tomb. This sense of newness and hope seemed to linger in the diminishing trail of smoke from the Lincoln funeral train as it departed station after station on its journey to Springfield, Illinois.

Today, the causes of the regional fracturing that led to the war—a war the likes of which the world had never witnessed—are still analyzed, but it was foremost about slavery. Attempts to deflect the causes toward violation of states' rights, taxes, and other issues ring hollow when pitted against a singular reality. If there had been no slavery, there would never have been a Civil War.

Slavery was not America's original sin; it was America's curse, left here by previous ruling nations. It had been necessary to incorporate it in some founding documents as a means of including slave-holding colonies in the newly formed United States of America, with the understanding that it would be dealt with once the nation was established. It was starting to die out on its own, but the invention of the cotton gin allowed for massive profits, and so the institution was reenergized in the South. Since the time of the Declaration of Independence, slavery had been a political can kicked down the road. Increasing regional hemorrhaging demanded the issue be dealt with. The matter was thrown in Lincoln's face like a bloody towel.

Lincoln went to Washington determined, foremost, to modernize the economy, and this could not include the expansion of slavery, especially into the developing western territories. Cognizant of the strides the country was making in the Industrial Revolution, he wanted to ensure that individual freedoms were protected so that all Americans could access opportunities. Unfortunately, some Southerners saw things differently. Seven states seceded shortly after his election with a singular cry: "He's going to take our slaves from us!"

The hope of abolitionists, Lincoln was repulsed by slavery—a horrid, immoral feudal system that generated tremendous wealth for a few. It was also economically impractical. Why, for example, did Northern railroads prosper and grow without slavery when Southern railroads, using essentially free labor, often ended up in financial straits?

Although the Civil War is examined primarily in terms of the period of the war itself (1861–1865), it is commonly accepted by historians that the Civil War era spanned 1850–1877. This includes the period known as Reconstruction. The war strained the nation financially, politically, morally, and spiritually as nothing had before or has since. It was a cataclysm that would have wrecked a lesser nation. The resilience of the nation should remain forever inspiring. The generation that fought to keep it united also preserved its daringly modern adventure in personal liberty. The people of that generation believed the country was noble. Their grief and suffering aside, they unflinchingly preserved and passed on the ideals of the country. They were, after all, the grandparents of World War II's "Greatest Generation."

But the horror of what transpired the night of Friday, April 14, 1865, would become almost genetically infused into future generations. Lee's surrender at Appomattox Court House, Virginia, on Sunday, April 9, had essentially put an end to hostilities. Those who saw Lincoln during that Friday remarked that he seemed the happiest they had ever seen him. This, of course, was because the tremendous weight of the war was now off his shoulders. That night, while he and First Lady Mary Todd Lincoln enjoyed a play at Ford's Theatre in Washington, DC (then called Washington City), a dashing young Maryland actor who was also an outlandish white supremacist shot Lincoln in the back of his head. The president died the following morning.

Horrified Northerners, most convinced the South sponsored the killing, had vengeful thoughts. But vengeance would have to wait. The martyred president would need a spectacular farewell, a funeral to rival that of the greatest emperor! The concept was vehemently opposed by his widow, who wanted his remains and those of their son, Willie, who had died of typhoid fever in 1862 at age eleven, quietly transported back to Springfield. In the end, she was badgered into relenting, and what followed was America's first national funeral, a spectacular event still regarded as the greatest event of its kind ever.

In my previous work for Westholme Publishing, *Railroads of the Civil War: An Illustrated History*, we rode by train across a war-gouged Southern landscape, glimpsing battlefields and wrecked cities. In this outing we will travel through the Northern countryside, again by train, allowing us to experience a land unblemished by war but emotionally devastated by the loss of its honored leader. Buildings draped in black cloth, flowered funeral arches soaring over tracks, bells tolling, volunteer bands playing dirges, and huge throngs of mourners are depicted in this book. Since my last writing, I have uncovered many forgotten photographs, which, combined with updated research—some of it myth busting—provide a much-needed reinterpretation of the event.

The funeral wasn't wholly about pageantry and romanticism. It was about dealing with intractable grief. Although folks gathered into crowds to express the nation's sorrow, the devastation felt on an individual level was exposed as well. This was true of many children who felt sadder about little Willie than the president.

Lincoln was admired for his commonness. He probably would have scoffed at such a pretentious farewell. He is continually rediscovered and reinterpreted by each generation. There is one thing certain about him, however, and it transcends even his own heavy-handedness at times: he was forever mindful of tyranny and America's vulnerability to it. He strides through history pounding his fist against the enemies of freedom. His words continue to be read by freedom seekers around the world.

He freed a race from slavery. It is hard to imagine how another American leader could have done it without such a brutal war, although other nations abolished it without bloodshed. But Lincoln was not going to preside over the breakup of the nation—no matter what the cost in lives.

Lincoln remains a remarkable example of self-improvement. Should America ever fall, it will leave a blueprint for future freedom fighters, shaped by Lincoln's impassioned defense of liberty. Americans need to heed his warnings more than ever. His call for a "new birth of freedom" in his Gettysburg Address and his warning in his 1862 message to Congress that, "We shall nobly save, or meanly lose, the last best hope of earth," may be prophetic.

ONE

"IT WAS A CRUEL, CRUEL HAND"

They wanted more, Abe and Mary Lincoln. His being just a top-notch Springfield lawyer wouldn't do. Driven, ambitious, they wanted much more. They wanted the big cities like Chicago, where they made a splash during the Lincoln-Douglas debates. They wanted to be the toast of Boston, New York, Atlanta, and especially Washington City, as the capital was called in those days. Mary, an intelligent but plain, troubled woman with a wicked temper and need to spite competing belles, pushed him to heights he may not have otherwise pursued. It turned out to be a dreadful case of "Be careful what you wish for."

Beyond keeping the nation united, their other signature agenda item—emancipation of America's slaves—resulted in over seven hundred thousand casualties, a trail of shattered Southern cities, and Abraham with a bullet through his brain. Nature itself seems to cry out the inevitable question, Why did it take such a catastrophic war to end slavery when other nations abolished it without bloodshed? Was war unavoidable? Could a more seasoned leader have figured out a more peaceful solution?

The Lincolns refused to dissolve into the ether of history. Among other things, they personify the modern dysfunctional family in many ways. In a time when "Spare the rod and spoil the child" was taken at face value, resulting in cruel beatings of children by parents, teachers, and employers, the Lincoln boys—little princelings affectionately declared by friends to be "notorious hellions"—were allowed to run wild and undisciplined at home, at their father's Springfield law office, and then at the White House. There may have been a lot of shouting and threatening, but neither parent had the heart to enforce any disciplinary actions let alone physically strike them.

There is little doubt that Mary Todd Lincoln was selfish, insecure, and eccentric. In his book *The Inner World of Abraham Lincoln*, Michael Burlingame quotes an unnamed federal official who had regular dealings with her as saying, "Mary Lincoln is like no other human being I ever saw. She is not easy to get along with though I succeed pretty well with her." He added, "She was of average height, weighing about a hundred and thirty pounds. She was rather compactly built, had a well-rounded face, rich dark brown hair, and bluish-gray eyes. In her bearing she was proud, but handsome and vivacious; she was a good conversationalist, using with equal fluency the French and English languages." He went on to describe her temperament: "Ordinarily she was affable and even charming in her manners; but when offended or antagonized she could be very bitter and sarcastic. In her figure and physical proportions, in education, bearing, temperament, history—in everything she was the exact reverse of Lincoln."

Today it is speculated she was bipolar, possibly suffered from schizophrenia, was neurotic or maybe had attention deficit disorder. Certainly she had compulsive disorders. Buying too much was among them. She nearly put Abraham into insurmountable and embarrassing debt. No matter how important her husband's meetings with his cabinet were, should a thunderstorm rage, she would send aides to bring him home to comfort her.

She was politically astute, promoting and supporting her husband at every point in his career even though it put her at odds with her Southern, Confederate-supporting family. Well aware of Abe's peculiar, often haphazard appearance (it's been said no one before or since has looked like him), she smartened him up in the latest fashionable dress. At the time of the first inaugural ride to Washington on a brightly colored train, she made sure he was properly dressed, knowing he would be meeting well-attired politicians along the way.

Unlike her husband, who lived an almost animal-like childhood on the frontier, Mary had been born into wealth and privilege. But as emotionally burdensome as she could be, she would have marched into hell for him. Petulant, self-absorbed, often graceless, Mary would wave her handkerchief in time with the band's playing, attempt an agreeable aspect, or fan herself frantically while pretending to be impressed by some windbag politician's discourse. Much of it was a necessary lie, the required conduct of a politician's wife who is expected to exalt her husband.

Abraham's appearance was revealed dazzlingly by an acquaintance, Dr. James Milner:

> His large bony face when in repose was unspeakably sad and as unreadable as that of a sphinx. His large eyes were as expressionless as those of a dead fish; but when he smiled or laughed at one of his own stories or that of another then everything about him changed; his figure became alert, a lightning change came over his countenance, his eyes scintillated and I thought he had the most expressive features I had ever seen on the face of a man.

During the darkest hours of the war, we wonder if, in the quiet of their chamber, Mary ever reached for him, pulled him close, and asked if there was anything she could do to help him. She had been good at wifely tenderness before the war. Life had since become oppressive and frightening. To comfort him now might require dismissing her own demands for constant attention. He, being needful but accepting of his wife's frailties, developed a skill at combating his depression with his own humor.

But we know she held him the night of April 14, 1865. She had been happy and coy with him at Ford's Theatre. But in an instant he was shot. She pulled him close, put her hand under his chin, and held up his head, trying to get him to breathe.

April 14, 1865—Good Friday—turned into one of America's most terrifying nights. An attempt was made to topple the federal government by killing the president, Vice President Andrew Johnson, and Secretary of State William H. Seward. The conspirators hoped it would excite the defeated Confederacy to revive its attempt at independence. The nation was beginning to accept the reality that its brutal war was finally over. Lee had surrendered to Grant only five days earlier, on April 9, 1865. The Confederacy was rapidly crumbling. But a fresh disaster had befallen the nation.

A talented young actor, John Wilkes Booth, a charismatic chap with a promising future and pretty fiancée, apparently had a dark side that got the better of him. Undone by the destruction of the Confederacy and being a wholehearted white supremacist and Confederate spy, he was rattled by a simmering hatred of Lincoln. Driven, he conspired with others to kill Lincoln, Johnson, and Seward. Booth would kill the president, Lewis Powell was to kill Seward, and George Atzerodt was to take out Johnson. Atzerodt got drunk and lost his nerve. Powell managed to enter Seward's house and savagely stab the secretary. He failed to kill him, however. The attack occurred almost at the same moment Lincoln was shot. The president died the following morning.

It turned out that Lincoln was murdered by a man he admired and endeavored to meet. The Lincolns frequented Ford's Theatre, and the president had been impressed with Booth. He invited him to the White House several times, but the disgruntled actor contrived excuses to refuse the invitations.

When the president and first lady attended the theater that Friday, they were tired but hopeful of being entertained by the play *Our American Cousin*. Joining them in the presidential box was army major Henry Rathbone and his fiancée, Clara Harris. General and Mrs. Ulysses S. Grant had been the Lincolns' original guests. Mrs. Lincoln and Mrs. Grant were not on good terms, but no matter. A family problem caused the Grants to cancel and board a train to their home in Philadelphia. Other friends were invited but could not make it. At the last minute, Henry and Clara accepted.

The Lincolns had enjoyed the day together. Folks around them said they appeared uncommonly happy. With the burden of the war lessening seemingly by the hour, they took a carriage ride and spoke of future plans. During the three previous nights, the president wrestled with terrible premonitions of being assassinated. Somehow he managed to push even those unpleasant thoughts away, allowing him to voice, for the first time in a long time, positive and hope-filled sentiments to his troubled wife. His deep love of her was beginning to resurface, having been suppressed, as were most of his joys, by the weight of the war.

Mary was downright coy and even playful later, at the theater, snuggling with him in the presidential box. Smiling, she asked Abe in a sly whisper, "What will Miss Harris think of me hanging on you so?" Abe dispelled her concern. "She won't think anything about it." It is believed those were the last words they ever spoke to each other.

The presidential box was actually two canopied end seats with a removable wall between them. It had been prepared for the Lincolns often. They arrived late, hurrying up the stairs with their guests. *Our American Cousin* was paused briefly so the orchestra could play "Hail to the Chief." That was followed with a vigorous standing ovation.

The assigned guard to the box was policeman John Frederick Parker. When intermission came, he slipped out of the theater and joined Lincoln's footman and coachman at a nearby saloon. Had Parker been at the box, it is doubtful he would have denied Booth entry to greet the Lincolns, so noted an actor was he. In any case, Booth gave a card to an usher who brought it to the presidential box. A moment later he was allowed entry into an outer area of the box. Once inside, he braced a stick against the inward-swinging door and proceeded to the door leading into the actual box. He peered through a peephole he had carved in the door earlier in the day.

Although Booth had never acted in that particular play, he knew it well. There was a line that generated the most laughs, and he waited for that, hoping the uproar would drown out the sound of his pistol shot. When actor Harry Hawk spoke the line—"Don't know the manners of good society, eh? Well, I guess I know enough to turn you inside out, old gal: you sockdologizing old man trap!"—the audience erupted in laughter. Booth pushed the door open, walked forward, and shot the president, who was also laughing, point blank in the back of his head. At the moment he was shot, Lincoln clenched Mary's hand. The bullet broke through the skull behind his left ear and plunged into his brain, lodging just above his right eye. Lincoln lurched forward in his rocking chair and then jerked back. Horrified, Mary reached for him and, realizing what had happened, screamed.

Major Rathbone, upon hearing the shot, lunged toward Booth to prevent his escape. Booth dropped his pistol, pulled out a knife, and attacked Rathbone. Seriously wounded, Rathbone persisted, grabbing Booth's coat as he was about to leap over the box and down onto the stage, roughly twelve feet below. During this grappling, Booth's right boot hit the framed portrait of George Washington hanging on the front of the box, and his spur became entangled in the Treasury Guard flag (a regimental flag of a Treasury Department-sponsored police unit) that was draped near it. This threw him off balance and he landed awkwardly, with his left foot turned under him. Many in the theater thought this was part of the play.

Booth pulled himself up and, limping across the stage, raised his bloody knife. With fiery passion he shouted an oath to the audience. It may have been "The South is avenged!" or a variation of that pronouncement. Some thought he screamed in Latin, "Sic semper tyrannis!" ("Thus always to tyrants!").

Mary and Clara's screams from the box together with Rathbone's shouting "Stop that man!" alerted the audience that something terrible had happened. Major Joseph B. Stewart was in the audience and bravely went into action, climbing over the orchestra pit and stage lights in pursuit of Booth. After a scrap with the orchestra leader, Booth escaped out the side door of the theater. His horse was being held by an unsuspecting fellow known as "Peanut Johnny." Booth struck him in the head with the back of his knife, got up on his horse, and gave the poor fellow a kick with his right leg. He then galloped off into the dim, oil-lit Washington night.

Inside the theater chaos erupted. A young actress in the play, Katherine M. Evans, glimpsed the president and said in an interview given in the 1900s, "I looked and saw President Lincoln unconscious, his head dropping on his breast, his eyes closed, but with a smile still on his face." Working through the crowd toward the presidential box was Charles Leale, a young army surgeon. He assumed the president had been stabbed, having seen blood dripping from Booth's knife during his dramatic exit. The outer door was still blocked when he got there, and Rathbone finally discovered the wooden brace and removed it.

When Leale entered, he saw Rathbone soaked with blood from a wound extending from his chest down the length of his left arm. There was another terrible slash down to the bone of the same arm. Leal passed him and found Lincoln stooped in his chair. Another doctor, Charles Sabin Taft, was lifted from the audience up into the box. Still suspecting Lincoln had been stabbed, probably in the shoulder, Leale and Taft cut away the collar of his shirt and ripped it open. Leale felt around the neck and shoulders, finding the bullet wound beneath the left ear. Amid Mary's hysterical shrieking, the two men managed to lower Lincoln to the floor of the box. Leale punctured a blood clot in the wound, allowing fluids and brain matter to escape. This resuscitated Lincoln, and he began to breathe. Leale allowed actress Laura Keene, who was performing in the play, to enter the box. She held the mortally wounded president's head in her lap. Knowing it was of little use, attending doctors continued to burst clots deep in the wound after he had been moved, keeping Lincoln alive another nine hours.

Head trauma experts today debate Lincoln's survivability. He certainly could not have survived in 1865, but were he rushed to a trauma center today, he might make it. He most likely would end up unstable on his feet, blind in his right eye, numb in parts of his body, incapable of clear thinking and possibly, after rehabilitation, able to speak to some extent. In short, he would suffer greatly. Had he, by some miracle, survived in 1865, it would have been a disaster to have such an incapacitated president during the harrowing reuniting of the country. Some experts familiar with such wounds believe the president was already dead when Leale reached him.

A third doctor, Albert King, arrived. With the help of some soldiers in the audience, the three doctors carried Lincoln across the street, under a soft rain, to the Petersen House, where he died. The doctors had decided a carriage ride to the White House would have been cruel for the dying president.

The shooting happened around 10:25 P.M. The .41-caliber slug fired from Booth's muzzle-loading derringer tore through the liquid-filled lateral ventricle, causing immediate brain hemorrhaging. Swelling likely began pressuring the brain stem and forcing the brain toward the spine. Lincoln was probably brain dead by midnight.

He had been placed diagonally in a bed too small for someone of his height. The room began to fill as news spread of the shooting.

The surgeon general of the US Army, Joseph K. Barnes, slowly inserted a metal probe into the wound until it tapped the back of the bullet. Lincoln's personal physician, Robert K. Stone, arrived.

Lincoln's oldest son, Robert, arrived around midnight. Son Thomas "Tad" was at Grover's Theatre delighting in *Aladdin and the Wonderful Lamp* when the play was interrupted and the manager announced the shooting to the audience. Tad was not allowed to join his mother and brother at the Petersen boardinghouse. Secretary of War Edwin Stanton and Secretary of the Navy Gideon Welles arrived. Stanton took charge, running the government throughout the night from the back parlor, receiving and sending telegrams, ordering pursuit of Booth and taking reports from witnesses. Inconsolable, Mary laid her head beside her husband's and pleaded for him to awaken and acknowledge her and their son. In his biography *Lincoln*, David Herbert Donald wrote that as her hysterical sobbing and shrieking heightened, Stanton forcefully demanded, "Take that woman out of here and do not let her back in here again!"

Dr. Leale stayed at the president's side most of the night. Despairing but eager to afford him the comfort of human touch, he held the dying man's hand. He later wrote in his report of the assassination, *Lincoln's Last Hours*, published in 1909, "sometimes, recognition and reason return just before departure. I held his hand firmly to let him know, in his blindness, that he had a friend." Then came that time when the recognition of human touch and voice dwindle and the human spirit moves into either oblivion or some divine realm. For Lincoln, that moment was officially recorded at 7:22 A.M., April 15, 1865. His personal secretary, John Hay, later remarked on witnessing Lincoln's last moment. In his work *Abraham Lincoln: A History*, published in 1890, he wrote, "a look of unspeakable peace came upon his [Lincoln's] worn features." Secretary Stanton spoke softly after those around the bed knelt in prayer, "Now he belongs to the ages." Some of those present later said it was "angels," not "ages."

Henry Rathbone married Clara Harris in 1867. In 1882, he was appointed US consul to the province of Hanover, Germany. His mental health had been steadily deteriorating, some said from his inability to prevent Lincoln's assassination. In 1883, while in Germany, he stabbed and shot Clara to death and then went after their children. House servants managed to get them safely away. He then tried to kill himself, stabbing himself repeatedly in the chest. Rathbone was committed to an asylum, where he died in 1911.

Booth's master plan had called for the assassination of Secretary of State William Seward. It was to occur that same night around 10:15, the time Booth expected to shoot the president. Seward had been thrown from his carriage April 5 and was suffering from a jaw broken in two places, a broken right arm, and a concussion. A special splint was fabricated to hold his jaw in place. Powell forced himself into the bedroom, punching and slashing his way past anyone who attempted to stop him. Pushing Seward's daughter violently away from his bed, Powell fell on Seward, stabbing him viciously in the face and neck. Amazingly, Seward survived the attack.

The assassination of Vice President Andrew Johnson was to occur at the Kirkwood House where Johnson was staying. This attack was slated for 10:15 P.M. as well, but George Atzerodt lost his nerve. He arrived at the Kirkwood that night but hit the downstairs saloon instead. Several hours later, he blundered into the street, drunk and frightened. He stumbled upon the Pennsylvania House Hotel around 2:00 A.M. and took a room.

Shortly after his escape from Ford's Theatre, Booth managed to talk guards at the Navy Yard Bridge into letting him cross. Civilians were forbidden to cross after 9:00 P.M. Fellow conspirator David Herold made it across the same bridge and into Maryland less than an hour later, which brings into question the need of having guards at the bridge at all. Herold caught up with Booth, and the two proceeded to Surrattsville, where they gathered weapons and supplies they had stored there. They then sought a local doctor, Samuel A. Mudd, to tend to Booth's leg. Mudd determined it was broken and bound a splint around it. He then fashioned a pair of crutches. Booth and Herold spent the night at the doctor's Maryland house and left in the morning with a hired local who would get them to predetermined locations. On April 24, they arrived at Richard H. Garrett's tobacco farm in Virginia. Booth convinced Garrett he was a wounded Confederate soldier and was therefore allowed to stay on the farm.

The news of the president's assassination spread quickly across the country, and it was understandably devastating. Just as the nation was preparing for reconciliation, this new disaster sank it into an almost unbearable darkness. It didn't seem possible such a terrible thing could have happened. In the capital, disbelief combined with rage and thoughts of vengeance. Dr. George Brainard Todd, who was in the audience at the time of the assassination, described the mood of Washingtonians in a letter to his brother Henry dated April 15: "Today all the city is in mourning, nearly every house being in black and I have not seen a smile, no business, and many a strong man I have seen in tears."

The South did not universally rejoice in the news. In some ways it seemed an ugly form of poetic justice. Southerners had to be careful in their conversations; their cities were under federal occupation, and anything disrespectful would be harshly dealt with.

The rebel president, Jefferson Davis, was simultaneously trying to revive a portion of the Confederacy, at least in the West, while getting his beloved wife, Varina, and three children to safety. He was concerned about his own survivability. Federal agents had been sent to either capture or kill him. That had been the situation most of the war. How ironic it must have seemed to Davis that a Confederate sympathizer was able to essentially stroll into a Washington theater and murder his archrival.

Federal efforts to get Davis had intensified since the fall of Richmond, Virginia. During those fateful, chaotic days, Davis made an impassioned farewell to Varina in the desperate hours he got his family out of the city. He stayed behind with a strong expectation he would not survive the fall of the Confederacy. He gave his wife a Colt pistol and a stash of bullets, telling her to do what she had to in the event of capture. Some Southerners were convinced Yankees were beasts who raped and murdered innocent Southern women. It was that kind of twisted romanticism that got their homeland into deep trouble in the first place. They rejected industrialism and most things modern, preferring to live in a fairy-tale past, even if that way of life required enslavement of other humans.

The Confederate president's world had begun to close in around him. His top general, Robert E. Lee, seemed to wash his hands of the whole adventure after informing Davis that Richmond was doomed. For four years, both sides went at each other's seats of power. Taking the enemy's capital meant certain victory. The North was victorious. Lincoln had entered Richmond and sat at Jefferson's desk. It was over.

Booth's terrible act may have briefly fanned the flames of resurgence in diehard Southern hearts, but even Lee threw water on that notion. When some of his troops begged him to fight on, he waved them off and, in calming tones, told them to accept reality—to go home to their families and start their lives anew.

Lincoln was not vengeful toward Davis. He even suggested Davis would do well to escape the country. Many Northerners believed Davis sponsored Lincoln's killing, and efforts to capture him increased, being combined under the tent of the manhunt for Booth and his conspirators. When Davis learned of the assassination, he did not welcome the news. He knew this would send even more hounds of hell after him.

Furthermore, the South was anticipating merciful treatment from Lincoln, who had said in his second inaugural address, "With malice toward none, with charity for all, . . . let us strive on to finish the work we are in, . . . to do all which may achieve and cherish a just and lasting peace among ourselves and with all nations." Those were among the most kind and healing words ever spoken by a conqueror. Lincoln's successor, Andrew Johnson, was not of the same caliber. He had been openly hostile and threatening to the South, urging Lincoln to be harsh in his postwar treatment. There were signs of it already, as Southerners were being ordered to show respect through memorial services, the tolling of bells, the closing of businesses, and no negative newspaper articles.

At the White House, Mary isolated herself in her bedroom, refusing to see just about everyone. Shattered and without her husband to settle her down, she sobbed uncontrollably. She could not bring herself to view her husband's remains, which were on display in the East Room. Likewise, she would not attend the Washington funeral. It was her wish that her husband's remains and those of their son Willie, who was in a vault in Georgetown's Oak Hill Cemetery, be taken quietly back to Springfield for burial.

The public would not accept such a simple farewell, however. Emotionally and physically weakened, Mary let herself be badgered into allowing what would be America's first national funeral, an unprecedented spectacle to rival that which might befit a king. Immediately, organizers readied the massive affair. It would involve a train carrying the remains from Washington to Springfield, with additional funerals held in larger cities along the route. Mary was depressed and disgusted by the whole thing but seemingly voiceless in the matter. She was haunted by dark fears, foremost the likelihood of rancid odors emanating from the decomposing bodies.

Her insistence that her husband's body be prepared by Dr. Charles Brown, the same embalmer used for Willie, was at least granted. Arriving at the White House, Brown employed the recently developed technique of opening an artery in the corpse, flushing out the blood with water, and then injecting a preservative, usually alcohol. George Alfred Townsend, a member of the press who viewed the body as it lay in state in the White House, gave a descriptive account:

> Approach and look at the dead man. Death has fastened into his frozen face all the character and idiosyncrasy of life. He has not changed one line of his grave, grotesque countenance, nor smoothed out a single feature. The hue is rather bloodless and leaden; but he was always sallow. The dark eyebrows seem abruptly arched; the beard, which will grow no more, is shaved close, save for the tuft at the short small chin. The mouth is shut, and like that of one who has put the foot down firm, and so are the eyes, which look as calm as slumber. The collar is short and awkward, turned over the stiff elastic cravat, and whatever energy or humor or tender gravity marked the living face is hardened into its pulseless outline. No corpse in the world is better prepared according to its appearances. The white satin around it reflects sufficient light upon the face to show that death is really there; but there are sweet roses and early magnolias, and the balmiest lilies strewn around, as if the flowers had begun to bloom even in his coffin.

He continued with lurid and grim details:

> Three years ago, when little Willie died, Doctors Brown and Alexander, the embalmers or injectors, prepared his body so handsomely that the President had it twice disinterred to look upon it. The same men, in the same way, have made perpetual these beloved lineaments. There is now no blood in the body; it was drained by the jugular vein and sacredly preserved, and through a cutting on the inside of the thigh the empty blood-vessels were charged with a chemical preparation which soon hardened to the consistence of stone. The long and bony body is now hard and stiff, so that beyond its present position it cannot be moved any more than the arms or legs of a statue. It has undergone many changes. The scalp has been removed, the brain taken out, and the chest opened and the blood emptied. All that we see of Abraham Lincoln, so cunningly calculated in this splendid coffin, is a mere shell, an effigy, a sculpture. He lies in sleep, but it is the sleep of marble. All that made

> this flesh vital, sentient, and affectionate
> is gone forever.

Union soldiers from the 16th New York Cavalry aggressively pursued Booth and Herold, arriving at Richard Garrett's Virginia farm on April 26. Four Union pursuers died before they got there. They drowned April 24 when their barge, the *Black Diamond*, collided with the steamer *Massachusetts* on the Potomac River. Because of that, it is safe to say that the soldiers who surrounded the tobacco barn where Booth and Herold were holed up were doubly mad. Herold surrendered, but Booth, ever the dramatic actor, was not going to be taken alive. A sergeant named Boston Corbett drew a bead on Booth through a crack in the barn wall and shot him in the back of the neck. The bullet entered about an inch below the spot where Booth's shot entered Lincoln's head. The bullet severed his spine, paralyzing him. He died two hours later. At one point he asked that his hands be lifted so he could see them. During the White House funeral, on April 19, the Reverend Doctor Phineas Gurley remarked in his powerful sermon:

> It was a cruel, cruel hand, that dark hand of the assassin, which smote our honored, wise, and noble President, and filled the land with sorrow. But above and beyond that hand there is another which we must see and acknowledge. It is the chastening hand of a wise and faithful Father. He gives us this bitter cup. And the cup that our Father hath given us, shall we not drink of it?

All but one of the plotters were captured and put on trial. The nation was insane with paranoia and conspiracy theories. Anyone remotely associated with any of the conspirators was put behind bars. Eight suspects were tried by military tribunal during a seven-week trial in which 366 witnesses testified. On June 30, a verdict of guilty came down. Lewis Powell, Mary Surratt, David Herold, and George Atzerodt were hanged in the Arsenal Penitentiary on July 7, 1865.

While the pursuit of the conspirators was under way, the spectacular funeral progressed. Millions would participate. Mary suffered alone at the White House a short time before being transported with her sons to Springfield. Although the public felt badly for her, Washington seemed to abandon her. It was time for her to go. Newspapers that had savaged her before, calling her a Confederate sympathizer when Southern papers called her a traitor now commented on her "frail sensitivity." The truth is, this last disaster left her fed up with Washington. She was eager to be free of the place. She had become the first in a terrible American sisterhood that would come to include Jacqueline Kennedy, Ethel Kennedy, and even Yoko Ono—women who witnessed the killing of the man they loved.

In this ambrotype taken May 25, 1858, by Samuel G. Alschuler, a determined Abraham Lincoln appears fit and elegant—his eyes set with ambition. The burden of war and personal tragedy would leave him haggard, aged, and almost unrecognizable from this image seven years later, just before he was murdered. (*Library of Congress*)

A warm and casual composition of the president with his son Tad. There is a suggestion of a grin on Lincoln's face. (*Library of Congress*)

Thomas Lincoln (1778–1851) was Abraham Lincoln's father. A family friend whose name was not recorded said he was, "An uneducated man; a plain, unpretending, plodding man," who was highly regarded by his neighbors. His wife, Nancy Hanks Lincoln—Abe's mother—died in 1818. Thomas then courted and married Sarah Bush Johnson. (*Library of Congress*)

Sarah Bush Johnson (1788–1869) was Abraham's stepmother. She married his father in 1818, bringing three children with her. (*Author's collection*)

The White House, or Executive Mansion, as it was often referred to, as it looked when the Lincoln family occupied it. (*Author's collection*)

An illustration from 1909 shows a more complete and happier Lincoln family. (*Library of Congress*)

An image taken in 1860 shows Mary Lincoln with sons Willie (left) and Tad. (*Author's collection*)

William Wallace "Willie" Lincoln died February 20, 1862, of typhoid fever. He was the Lincoln's third son. The boys were affectionately referred to as "notorious hellions." They turned their father's Springfield, Illinois, law office upside down with their antics and did the same at the White House. Willie's death was devastating for the family. Mary had his casket removed from Oak Hill Cemetery in Georgetown and placed on the funeral train with his father's remains for burial in Springfield. (*Author's collection*)

Ford's Theatre in Washington, DC, or Washington City as it was called then, is grimly decorated in mourning after the president's assassination April 15, 1865. The owner permanently closed the theater after the funeral. (*Library of Congress*)

A Currier and Ives illustration of the assassination has events slightly out of order. Major Henry Rathbone reacted to John Wilkes Booth after the shot was fired. (*Author's collection*)

Major Henry Rathbone and his fiancée, Clara Harris, were guests of the Lincolns' the night of the assassination. Rathbone seized Booth after the fatal shot. Booth freed himself by stabbing Rathbone's left arm. The major's mental health began to decline after the assassination, owing, many believed, to his inability to prevent the killing. Appointed US consul to the province of Hanover in 1882, he relocated to Germany. On April 14, 1883, he stabbed and shot his wife to death and then attacked their children. Servants got them away. Rathbone then stabbed himself five times in the chest. He survived and was put in an asylum, where he died August 14, 1911. (*Library of Congress*)

Noted photographer of the day Mathew Brady took this photo of the presidential box in Ford's Theatre two days after the assassination. (*Library of Congress*)

Charles Leale, a young army surgeon, was the first doctor to reach the president, being let into the box by Rathbone. Leale resuscitated the president even though he knew the wound was mortal. (*Library of Congress*)

Actress Laura Keene (born Mary Francis Moss) was performing in the play *Our American Cousin* when Lincoln was shot. She worked her way into the presidential box, where Leale allowed her to cradle the mortally wounded president's head in her lap. (*Library of Congress*)

After being shot the night of April 14, 1865, Lincoln was taken across the street to the Petersen House, an 1849 Federal style row house then serving boarders. The president died at 7:22 A.M. the following day, at age fifty-six. (*Author's collection*)

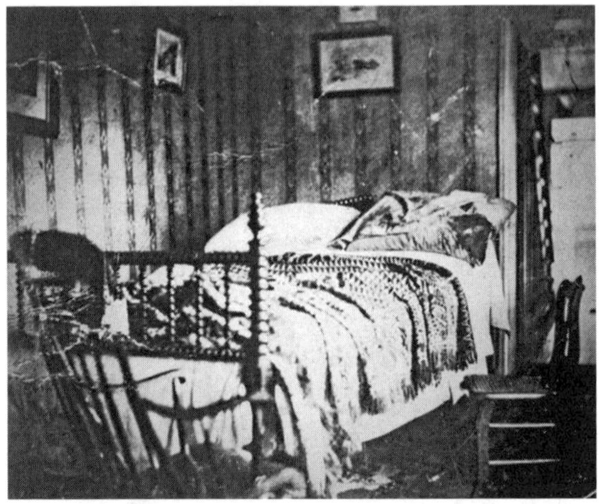

The bed in the Petersen House where Lincoln died. (*Author's collection*)

Lincoln on his death bed drawn by Hermann Faber, an artist on the surgeon general's staff. (*Library of Congress*)

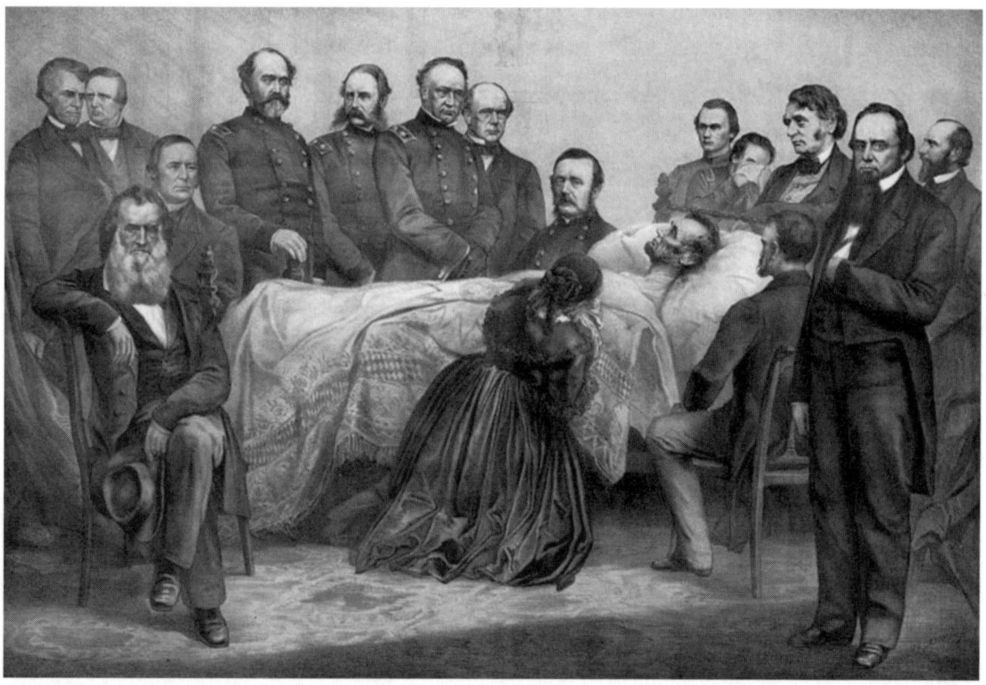

Grief stricken, Mary Lincoln anguishes in her husband's last moments in this poignant illustration. (*Author's collection*)

It was truly a night of horror for America as conspirators attempted to bring down the federal government. At almost the same moment Lincoln was shot, Lewis Powell burst into Secretary of State William H. Seward's bedroom, pushed his daughter away, and stabbed him. The disfigurement caused by the attack is evident in the photo to the right. It was the only photo Seward allowed to be taken of him the rest of his life. (*Author's collection*)

The clothing Lincoln wore the night he was killed. (*Library of Congress*)

Vice President Andrew Johnson would be sworn in as president shortly after the announcement of Lincoln's death. (*Library of Congress*)

The reward poster for the conspirators was bold, with red, blue, and black lettering. Actual photos of the men were pasted on the broadsides. (*Library of Congress*)

The assassin, John Wilkes Booth, was a member of a prominent American theatrical family and an accomplished actor in his own right. A Marylander with strong Confederate sympathies, he was aggressively tracked down and killed April 26, 1865. (*Library of Congress*)

Booth's brother Edwin, pictured with his daughter, Edwina, was an actor as well. A far more decent man, Edwin saved Lincoln's son Robert from serious injury or possible death not long before the assassination. It happened on a train station platform in Jersey City, New Jersey. The press of passengers forced young Robert to steady himself against a car on the track. When the car moved, Robert was pulled around and began to fall into the space between the car and the platform. Edwin seized him by the collar and pulled him to safety before he fell beneath the car's wheels. (*Library of Congress*)

A prewar image of a slave auction in Easton, Maryland. Although a slave state, it grudgingly stayed with the Union. Never Lincoln country—the president lost there in both elections—Maryland was the home of his assassin. The state kicked in $10,000 to the reward fund for Booth's capture. (*Author's collection*)

Boston Corbett was the Union Army soldier who shot and killed Booth. It happened at a tobacco barn on the Virginia farm of Richard Garrett. (*Author's collection*)

First Lady Mary Lincoln dressed in mourning for her son Willie, who died in 1862. It is believed she wore this same dress while mourning her husband. (*Author's collection*)

Charles Forbes was a messenger and assistant to the Lincolns. He was with the presidential party the night of the assassination. During intermission he went to a nearby saloon for a drink with John Parker, one of Lincoln's guards. This allowed John Wilkes Booth to enter the theater and kill Lincoln. Mary Lincoln included Forbes among those she held responsible and never forgave him. (*Author's collection*)

The Reverend Doctor Gurley was chaplain of the US Senate as well as a personal friend of and spiritual adviser to the president. He and his wife, Emma, visited the White House frequently. He counseled Lincoln when, in deep grief over the loss of Willie, the president began to doubt his own faith. He stayed at Lincoln's bedside the night of the shooting and later preached the funeral sermon at the White House.
(*Author's collection*)

The Reverend Doctor Phineas Densmore Gurley, pastor of New York Avenue Presbyterian Church, which the Lincolns attended, gives an impassioned sermon beside the catafalque in the White House, April 19, 1865. (*Author's collection*)

This is the funeral car that transported Lincoln's casket from the White House to the Capitol, where the president's body lay in state. (*Library of Congress*)

A bold portrait of Admiral David Glasgow Farragut, whose famous battle cry during the August 1864 Battle of Mobile Bay, "Damn the torpedoes and full speed ahead!," endures in modern culture. He was a pall-bearer during the funeral. (*Library of Congress*)

Federal buildings, the feeling of newness still about them, are decorated for the funeral obsequies. (*Author's collection*)

A group of prominent Washington citizens is seated beneath the portico of the Treasury Building, awaiting the funeral cortege. The columns of the building are adorned with mourning bands. (*Author's collection*)

Bands of black fabric, flags, and a portrait of Lincoln embellish the Senate chamber in the Capitol during the funeral. (*Author's collection*)

Top: The funeral procession down Pennsylvania Avenue was a spectacular affair. Americans had never seen anything like it. (*Library of Congress*) Bottom: The assassination and funeral drew the attention of the world. The *London News* provided the British a sense of the spectacle in Washington with this remarkable illustration. (*Author's collection*)

Crowds line the procession route. There are onlookers on rooftops. Note the buildings decorated in black bunting. (*Library of Congress*)

The trial of the conspirators over, it was time for justice to be served. The ropes are being adjusted around their necks. From left are Mary Surratt, Lewis Powell, David Herold, and George Atzerodt. At 1:26 P.M. on July 7, 1865, the four condemned conspirators were hanged in the yard of Washington's old Arsenal Penitentiary. (*Library of Congress*)

TWO

"TEARS OF RAIN FELL"

The North was now saturated with a morose expectation of the funeral. It was to be carried out via train and telegraph, the two modern contrivances that navigated the country into a massive industrial era. The railroad was the backbone of the country. It altered cities, opened territories, and gave birth to numerous technologies, creating thousands of jobs. Enormous profits were earned during the war, laying the groundwork for future rail barons.

It was also the railroad that had led to, escalated, and prolonged the terrible carnage of the war. It was the first time railroads were used extensively in a major conflict. The logistics of battle changed dramatically. Previously, armies marched to battle, encumbered with slow-moving beasts of burden. The farther an army traveled from its base, the more precarious its situation. Now railroads could rush soldiers and supplies in ten times faster. Most of the deadliest battles in the war were fought around railheads.

Lincoln was a railroad man through and through. His greatest legislative accomplishment as president was the Transcontinental Railroad, which would go into full service in 1869. He used it to seduce the West into remaining loyal to the Union. As far back as 1832, during Lincoln's first bid for the Illinois Senate, he called for better transportation, saying "no other improvement that reason will justify us in hoping for can equal in utility the railroads." As a prairie lawyer he sought railroad cases, charging as little as $10 for defaulting stock subscribers and land-variance issues, but he earned $5,000 for a case brought to the Illinois Supreme Court. His participating in several cases helped establish precedents that led to far-reaching improvements in railroads.

Because they were well used during the war, the railroads were adept at quick mobilization, and the lines used in the funeral rapidly planned routes, schedules, and many other details needed to pull off the massive endeavor. The funeral train was officially designated the Lincoln Special. The railroads used were placed under military control, and the War Department drew up the final route. The approximately 1,654-mile route essentially retraced the path taken by Lincoln's 1861 inaugural train, with a few deviations. General Daniel McCallum, who brilliantly managed the US Military Railroads agency during the war, oversaw the entire operation. Secretary of War Stanton was fundamentally involved and handpicked General Edward D. Townsend as commander. Townsend traveled with the train from beginning to end, sending reports back to Stanton.

The train that would carry Lincoln back to Springfield began to excite the public as much as the chance of glimpsing the president's remains. Observing the magnificent high-end cars, adorned in black bunting and drawn by a polished locomotive decorated with flags, stirred the imagination.

Without question, the star of the train was a newly built luxury car intended for Lincoln's use named the United States. Constructed in the car shops of the Orange & Alexandria Railroad in Alexandria, Virginia, it was the best-appointed car in the country. It was intended for transporting the president, and his family when necessary, on official business. It was a mobile headquarters—the Air Force One of its day. There would be a lot of travel, no doubt, after the war, with the president meeting with governors and other dignitaries. The interior was convertible. It had a parlor and four lounges, two of which could be combined into a sleeping compartment to accommodate the tall president.

What the exterior color was has been debated. A surviving relic of the car, a window frame, had a remnant of paint that was subjected to lab analysis. The color was determined to be a deep maroon. But could this have been a repainted color? As we will learn from one of the primary builders of the car, it was originally painted a deep olive.

In most photos, the car looks to be a deep, dark color. The wet collodion film process of the day sometimes registered colors lighter or darker than they actually were. A medium or dark olive tone could then look very dark, where a dark color could show as a medium gray. Whatever the color, delicate pinstriping added to its striking appearance. The original design called for two wheel sets, or trucks, but it was decided four would make for a smoother ride. There are accounts, however, of the car having difficulty going through switches during the funeral run, and the extra-wide wheels tended to make the car shift from side to side.

An enduring myth claims that Lincoln was opposed to the car being built in the first place, complaining that it was too expensive and pretentious in a time of war. It seems likely that if the president didn't want it built, he would have stopped the project. He believed the nation should continue with its projects as a way of keeping morale up. An example of this was his insistence that work on the unfinished Capitol continue, although the press criticized it as too costly a project during wartime.

One of the primary builders of the private car was James T. Barkley. He later moved to San Diego, and in a newspaper interview, he provided firsthand information as to Lincoln's thoughts on the car. The interview, published in the *New York Times* on February 12, 1910, read in part:

> "In December 1863 I was detailed, on recommendation of General McCallum, by General Thomas Holt, to build a new car for the President" said Mr. Barkley. Assisted by a civilian and an enlisted mechanic, Barkley said he went to work

in a room in the government shops at Alexandria, VA.

"Lincoln would visit us two or three times a month during construction," said Mr. Barkley. "Sitting on a sawhorse, he would suggest changes. There were many suggestions. In the rear of the car was a conference room. In the middle was Lincoln's quarters; in the front a washroom. The car was upholstered in red plush. The work was finished in the third week of May."

Eleven months later, Barkley said, the car, heavily draped and bearing Lincoln's body in a sealed casket, moved out of Washington for Illinois.

Another myth is that Lincoln never rode the car while alive. In the book *The Assassination of Lincoln: The Funeral Car*, a newspaper interview with another of the key builders tells a different story. Myran H. Lamson was the enlisted mechanic Barkley mentioned, and he was also superintendent of the Orange & Alexandria Railroad, serving as director during construction of the car. Lawrence O'Day was the civilian builder Barkley referred to. In the article, Lamson explained:

> A room was partitioned off in the car shop and no one was allowed to enter except to bring material. The car had double trucks with broad tread wheels to enable it to run over nearly all railroads in the United States. The color, when finished, was a dark olive with a large oval panel on either side, in which was painted the United States coat of arms. This car was finished and run out over the Orange & Alexandria Railroad on a trial trip to Warrenton and pronounced a perfect success. On the trial trip were President Lincoln, Secretary of State Seward, Gen. McCallum who had charge of all military railroads in the United States.

Lamson, O'Day, and Barkley were also along on that ride.

We would do well to trust Lamson's accounts on this matter. He was intimately involved with the car from its design to completion. He also helped alter the car to accept the president's casket, fashioning rollers so it could easily slide into and out of the car. The ornamental hand railings on the platform were removed so the casket could be moved more efficiently. Lamson built the pyramid-shaped bier upon which the casket rested in the car. There was a railing around the top of it. A faithful attendant during the funeral, he traveled in the officers car, which was for civilian and military men chosen to accompany the train, and often stood as a guard of honor over Lincoln's remains.

Lincoln's corpse was removed from the Petersen House and taken by hearse to the White House for preparation. A small cortege led by bareheaded army officers and an escort of soldiers took care of this. The casket, resting on a bier, was covered with a US flag. Shocked citizens lined F Street, watching the sad procession. Noah Brooks, a Washington correspondent for the *Sacramento Union*, wrote in his book *Washington in Lincoln's Time*:

> Instantly all flags were raised to half-mast all over the city, the bells tolled solemnly and with incredible swiftness Washington went into deep, universal

mourning. All shops, government departments and private offices were closed, and everywhere, on the most pretentious residences and on the humblest hovels, were the black badges of grief. Nature seemed to sympathize in the general lamentation, and tears of rain fell from the moist and somber sky. The wind sighed mournfully through the streets crowded with sad-faced people, and the broad folds of funeral drapery flapped heavily in the wind over the decorations of the day before.

As the little cortege passed down the street to the White House, every head was uncovered, and the profound silence which prevailed was broken only by the sobs and by the sound of the measured tread of those who bore the martyred President back to the home which he had so lately quitted full of life, hope, and cheer.

In cities and towns across the North, governors and mayors addressed the citizens and called for, among other things, businesses to be closed, buildings to be draped in mourning, and memorial services to be held simultaneously with the April 19 funeral at the White House. This was four days after the killing.

The East Room catafalque loomed over the casket. It was fifteen feet tall with four pillars supporting a domed canopy of black cloth. There were flowered wreaths and floral arrangements throughout the room. The walls were heavily draped in black cloth. The new president, Andrew Johnson, was present much of the time. Tad and Robert Lincoln were holed up in their mother's bedroom, captives in a sense, for she wouldn't let them attend the viewing. Grief stricken, their anguish was made worse by their mother's wailing. She did, however, relent and allow them, for a time, to join the group of designated mourners positioned near the catafalque. The party included household members and personal secretaries.

While mourners filed past the casket, behind the scenes the multitude of details for the national event were being frantically worked out. Telegrams were coming in from governors pleading to have the train come through their states. This was particularly true of New England states that felt entitled because of their strong antislavery tradition. Stanton rejected all requests, emphatic that no changes could be made to the route.

The White House funeral ended with the Reverend Gurley's sermon. Outside the mansion, an impressive hearse, a kind of moving altar, was hitched to six white horses waiting to take the casket to the Capitol for more viewing. Fifty thousand soldiers and many bands were arranged in order for the procession. Fifty thousand onlookers lined the procession route. Union cavalry officer William Gamble, who had been at Ford's Theater the night of the assassination, wandered into the streets that day, observing the procession from different vantages. He registered his impressions in a letter to his wife, Frederika, dated April 21, 1865. A portion of the letter, related in the online Abraham Lincoln's Classroom article "The Funeral Train of Abraham Lincoln," reads:

> It seemed as if a million of the people had assembled and Washington was a living mass of human beings of all kinds, shades and colors. I have never dreamed of such a sight before and never expect to witness

> such an assembly again. It seemed as if the judgment day had taken place and all the people were congregated together, cavalry, infantry, artillery, miles in length, besides citizens without number.

Noah Brooks, ever observant and articulate, related in his writings about the procession up Pennsylvania Avenue, under way at 2:00 P.M., that the city was jammed with mourners. Bells tolled and minute guns fired constantly at all the forts surrounding the city. He wrote in *Washington in Lincoln's Time*:

> The day was cloudless, and the sun shone brilliantly upon cavalry, infantry, artillery, marines, associations, and societies, with draped banners and accompanied in their slow march by mournful dirges from numerous military bands. . . . One noticeable feature of the procession was the appearance of colored societies which brought up the rear, humbly, as was their wont.

The three-mile-long procession took a little over two hours to reach the Capitol. The casket was brought into the rotunda and prepared for public viewing. When the doors were opened, a continuous stream of mourners ascended the Capitol steps to the eastern entrance of the rotunda, passing the casket at the rate of thirty-five hundred per hour. Guards marshaled the crowd into two lines that separated at the foot of the casket. After passing, the two lines joined again and exited through the front doors, emerging under the massive portico.

Many felt the need to involve themselves more deeply in the event. While passing the flower-strewn casket, which was open at the top, some cried loudly or fell to painful sobbing. Some shouted angry oaths about the assassin and voiced fiery indignation about the whole affair. A guard stood at the head of the casket to make sure no one touched it.

Just up the street from the Capitol, at the Baltimore & Ohio (B&O) Railroad station on Jersey Avenue, arrangements were being made for the funeral train's departure. General Townsend assumed his responsibility for the train. The United States and the officers car were fully prepared. The officers car—intended for members of the president's family, the congressional committee assigned to make the journey, and mechanics—was lent by the Philadelphia, Wilmington & Baltimore Railroad. It was a handsome affair, with a parlor, chamber, water tanks, gasometer, kitchen, and dining room.

Willie Lincoln's casket had already been removed from its small vault and placed inside the United States. At one point along the journey, a crewman claimed the casket had been placed in the baggage car. It is generally believed, however, that it was always in the United States with his father's casket.

A small procession brought the president's remains to the train station and waited while it was put aboard. After it was placed on Lamson's custom-built bier, a large black cloth was placed over it and two straps were fastened to hold everything in place. Several thousand troops were in line beside the railroad. When the train rolled out, many of them—including those who had witnessed the war's bloodiest horrors—bowed their heads and wept pitifully. It was a spontaneous and heartbreaking scene. The week had been a nightmare—the president murdered here in Washington, blood-stained pillowcases, his languishing death, and poor Mary and the boys! It was too much.

A pilot train of a locomotive and one car would always precede the Lincoln Special by ten minutes. The purpose was to make sure all was clear ahead, especially at crossings where crowds tended to gather. B&O locomotive no. 239 pulled the pilot train out of the Jersey Avenue station at 7:50 A.M., April 21. At 8:00 A.M., the funeral train rolled out, driven by engineer Thomas Beckett. It steamed into the fresh spring morning air amid the tolling of church bells.

The funeral train was pulled by B&O's no. 238 locomotive, the Edwin H. Jones, a highly polished American standard 4-4-0, the workhorse of most railroads. It was brand new, built in 1865 in the prestigious Thatcher-Perkin shops. A colorful, balloon-stacked beauty, it featured brass boiler rings and a metallic gray-toned Russian boiler jacket. Russian metal workers had developed a technique to slow the rusting of iron boiler jackets by pounding graphite into them, thus forming a coating. The iron was then polished to a high luster, giving the locomotive a dazzling appearance.

Locos were moving, breathing works of art. The tenders often featured hand-painted frescoes or elaborate gold leaf floral patterns. The Edwin H. Jones was decorated with flags and crepe, making it even more impressive. It pulled eight cars, all neatly attired in mourning cloth. Robert Lincoln was aboard, accompanied by four relatives: John Ninian Wirt Edwards (husband of Elizabeth Todd), Clark M. Smith (husband of Ann Todd), Brigadier General John Blair Smith Todd (son of Dr. John Todd and Elizabeth Smith), and Charles Alexander Smith (brother of Clark M. Smith). Robert Lincoln took the train to Baltimore and then returned to help comfort his mother.

Stops at Relay and Annapolis Junction were made during the thirty-eight-mile trip to Baltimore. Most trains of that day could travel twenty miles on a load of wood and a tender full of water. Piles of wood for the Lincoln Special were often left by the trackside, like an offering.

The train arrived at Baltimore's Camden Station at 10:00 A.M. A hearse brought the body to the rotunda of the Merchant's Exchange, where thousands viewed it. Again the streets were packed with mourners. Marylanders never wasted any love on Lincoln, but the killing nonetheless shocked them. How could they not feel bad for Mary and the boys? Baltimore, now in loyal Union hands, experienced awkward and remorseful feelings. John Wilkes Booth was from Baltimore. The city kicked in $10,000 to the reward fund for his capture.

While Lincoln lay in state, the train was reconfigured and readied for the trip to Harrisburg, Pennsylvania. It came into Baltimore on the B&O but would leave from the Northern Central Railroad Calvert Street station. The funeral and officers cars were hauled to it over a street railroad, of which there were many in those days. Some witnesses said mules pulled the cars. The guests on the train were transferred to different passenger and sleeper cars. Each railroad had to supply its own cars, and they had to be their best. Hours had been spent cleaning, touching up, stitching frayed upholstery, and polishing brass. And that was before yards of black cloth were draped along the tops of the windows. The hearse brought the casket to the station, and at 3:00 P.M. the special rolled out, its bell clanging and whistle announcing its approach to crossings.

The number of passengers is repeatedly estimated at three hundred. Classified as mourners, they included family members, friends, delegates, mechanics, security men, and politicians, and they were all males. It seems unlikely there were three hundred. Of the eight-car train, one was a baggage car, one was the funeral car, and one was the officers car. That would leave five cars to accommodate three hundred mourners and crewmen. Most mid-nineteenth-century cars could seat up to forty-six. The train was rearranged along the way, but there always seems to have been at least two sleeper cars. Sleepers generally couldn't handle as many passengers as a coach.

One railroad employee involved with the train when it left Washington said there were about eighty-five additional people joining the crew and officers. Railroad men were pretty good at gauging crowds. The number probably varied between one hundred and one hundred fifty. Women's groups, churches, benevolent societies, and restaurants provided meals along the way. It would have been daunting for the railroads and committees present at the smaller stations to feed three hundred at a time. Another consideration is that large delegations, including mayors, governors, senators, and all their hangers-on boarded the train in each state it passed into. There had to be room for them.

On both sides of the tracks, and for most of the route, onlookers waited, caught up in the mania sweeping the country. There was a compulsion to somehow be a part of the event. Many warmed themselves against the cold night air beside bonfires. As the train traveled across a stricken nation, the dark countryside was almost medieval, illuminated with bonfires, campfires, and torches.

The appearance of the pilot train sent hearts to pounding because that meant the funeral train was only ten minutes behind. The train ran slowly, allowing a lingering view. Men took off their hats and held them over their hearts. Small children were held up and told to remember what they saw. Faces were awash in tears.

Upon crossing the state line into Pennsylvania, the train picked up the state's governor, Andrew Curtain, and some other dignitaries. That was around 5:30 P.M. The information that the governor had ridden the train through his state was quickly telegraphed ahead, and it became the practice for other governors when the train entered their state. A brief stop was made at York. The ladies of the town placed a large floral wreath on the casket.

A heavy rain was falling when the train arrived in Harrisburg at 8:20 P.M. Fifteen hundred soldiers had been waiting in that rain for over an hour. The casket was put into a hearse, and a large military escort led it through the streets to the statehouse. As was the case along the entire venue, bells tolled, military bands played dirges, choirs sang, and guns were fired. The passengers left the cars and were guided to wherever meals had been prepared for them.

Harrisburg's streets were jammed as never before. Families from surrounding towns and suburbs made predawn trips in buggies. At the beautiful Italianate station, the honor guard kept dutiful watch over the car. Each city was expected to provide guards. All stations were decorated to some extent. In many, additional candles and lamps were set among pine garlands, flags, and strands of black and white cloth. If there were any locomotive headlamps available, they were brought inside, their reservoirs filled with oil and their wicks lit. Sometimes the hands of the large railroad wall clocks, so depended on by passengers, were locked at 7:22 A.M., the time the president died. There were bouquets of fragrant spring flowers inside and out. Crosses, shields, and wreaths, all wonderfully bedecked with flowers, were placed on stands.

There are no interior photographs of any of these stations. Few photographers were skilled at interior image taking. Their studios had large, north-facing windows and skylights to facilitate portrait taking, but stations tended to be dark. Noted photographer Mathew Brady was capable of making complex interior images, but he was not assigned to accompany the train.

The limits of photographic technology of the day left an inadequate photographic legacy of the funeral. In so many cases, the train arrived or departed late at night or in predawn darkness, preventing decent images.

Gloomy rain seemed to follow the train, as if bent on adding to the sadness. It, too, presented photographers with problems. Long exposure under dim, gray skies resulted in blurred images.

Some stationmasters had extra oil lamps and torches put out on the platforms to provide additional illumination. Locomotives were brought up and their headlamps lit. More gas lamps were added, and the red light of signal lanterns lent a sense of mystery. Gas-lit lampposts threw eerie yellow light across the mourners. The application of mourning bunting, flowers, and flags, both inside and out, was meticulous and done with a sense of balance and design. This was a preoil America powered by wood, coal, gas, and whale oil. The odor of whale-oil lamps filled stations. The precious commodity was also used to polish the locomotives' brass trimmings to a high luster.

As events were telegraphed ahead, funeral committees pursued efforts to outshine previous stops, and last-moment enhancements were made. At one stop, large mirrors were provided so mourners could see both sides of the train. Clearly, a competition was evolving—a kind of morbid, postmortem art form that included theatrics and staging.

Throughout the pageant, Southerners became increasingly outraged. They believed the lavish funeral was a slap in their faces and a way to implicate the entire South in the killing. There were Southerners who felt terrible about Lincoln's death. As a whole, however, they found the unending display of the corpse morbid and disgusting.

At Harrisburg, the casket was put on display in the hall of the House of Representatives. Two lines began to file by in a slow, continuous stream. Back at the station, the train was again reworked. The doors at the statehouse were closed at midnight, leaving thousands still waiting in line. Viewing was allowed for a short time the following morning. An escort returned the casket to the station, and at 10:00 A.M., Saturday, April 22, the train rumbled out, its flags, wreaths, and strands of bunting fluttering in the cool morning air. The engineer, fireman, and wood passer—all well dressed, usually in black suits—were honored by this opportunity. They kept their locos running safely and smoothly. The inside of the cab, usually an oily, sooty mess, had been cleaned. The brass gauges had been buffed to a shine the way a marksman lovingly polishes the metal on a fine rifle. The glass gauge covers were cleaned as well, with the enameled faces, black numbers, and dials showing smartly inside.

Pennsylvania Railroad locomotive no. 331, with engineer John E. Miller at the throttle, chugged slowly and with solemn pride past thousands of grieving folks along the tracks. Mourners gathered in tight, dark groups at Middletown, Elizabethtown, Mount Joy, Landisville, and Dillerville. In Lancaster, roughly twenty thousand lingered at the station. A sign read, "Abraham Lincoln, the Illustrious Martyr of Liberty: the nation mourns his loss; though dead he still lives." Former president James Buchanan was in town and watched with many others as Congressman Thaddeus Stevens spoke a tribute.

The whistle and bell announced approaches to Penningtonville, Parkesburg, Coatesville, Gallagherville, Downington, Oakland, and West Chester. At 4:30 P.M., tired, panting, and with its bell clanging, no. 331 reached Philadelphia's Wilmington & Baltimore Railroad station on Broad Street.

Although the train arrived over an hour ahead of schedule, two hours passed before the casket was removed from the car for the procession to Independence Hall. The hearse was magnificent. Like many used during the funeral, it had black bunting and sported a fringed, lined canopy and many silver-toned fittings. Plumes of black and white feathers sprouted from the top. Eight black horses gave an imperial flare to the cortege.

An estimated five hundred thousand people—seemingly the entire population of Philadelphia—crowded the streets, hoping to catch a glimpse of the procession. It was a bright, sunny day when the train arrived, but the procession didn't get started until after 7:00 P.M. The city was dark when the remains arrived at the grounds of Independence Hall. The privileged of the city were allowed to view the remains first, having been given special invitation cards. That had been the procedure in many cities, but it caused unrest here. Average citizens were consigned to long lines while those in the social hierarchy were given immediate access. Viewing for cardholders was from 10:00 P.M. to 1:00 A.M.

The doors were opened the next day, Sunday, April 23, at 5:00 A.M. Many in the nearly three-mile-long line had been awake since the previous morning, and tempers again began to flare. Pickpockets and thugs worked the crowd. Mobs comprising the general public pushed beyond the guide ropes intended to advance them in orderly rows toward the entrance of Independence Hall. The ropes were cut, and police looked on helplessly as chaos ensued. Fights broke out. Hats and bonnets went flying. Punches were thrown. Women's dresses were literally pulled off. Amid screams of pain and profanities, people were trampled and shoved, resulting in broken limbs.

Finally, order was established, and the riled crowd was allowed to view the president throughout the day and night until 1:00 A.M. Monday morning. As many as three hundred thousand may have filed past the casket, with thousands left behind.

The casket was positioned in the center hall, and Philadelphians felt it would be a nice touch to place the Liberty Bell at Lincoln's head. Mourners could then read its inscription, "Proclaim Liberty throughout all the land, and unto all the inhabitants thereof." Eighteen candelabras with burning wax tapers lit the room. The sound of somber music being played around the city could be heard, in muffled tones, along with incessant bell tolling and cannon blasts. Lincoln's prophetic words, spoken during his inaugural visit to Independence Hall in 1861, were in the thoughts of many. He spoke of how dear the Declaration of Independence was to him and how the principle of equal opportunity for all was fundamental to the nation's survival. He then said something dark. "But if this country cannot be saved without giving up that principle . . . I would rather be assassinated on this spot than surrender it." When the casket was removed from the hall at 2:30 A.M., the room was left open so citizens could at least see where the president had lain in state.

During the night, the train moved from the West Philadelphia station to the Kensington station of the Philadelphia & Trenton Railroad. Mules towed the United States from the West Philly station to the tracks along the Schuylkill River. The procession to the P&T station was peaceful. Hundreds of citizens held candles and shivered in the cold morning air as the hearse clattered on Philly's cobbled streets.

Locomotive no. 331 pulled out of the Kensington station at approximately 4:00 A.M. Large crowds watched silently as it reached Bristol, Pennsylvania, and Morristown, New Jersey. After a quick servicing stop at Trenton, it was off to Princeton, New Brunswick, Rahway, Elizabeth City, and Newark. In its coverage of the Trenton stop, the *New York Times* referred to the United States' color as "strong crimson." Telegraph lines around the country hummed with details of the extraordinary funeral, transforming Lincoln, reviled by many in life, into something divine: America's saint.

At Jersey City, New Jersey, a vast choir composed of German musical associations overwhelmed the delegates accompanying the president. Apparently, this happened in the huge train shed there. In his book *Abraham Lincoln: His Great Funeral Cortege, from Washington City to Springfield, Illinois, with a History and Description of the National Lincoln Monument*, a chronicler of the funeral, J. C. Power, wrote, "As they chanted an anthem or requiem for the dead, many who were unused to weeping were affected to tears."

The link and pin couplers of the United States were disconnected, and the car rolled onto a steam lighter—a barge—and ferried across the Hudson River to the Debrosses Street ferry in Manhattan. The German choir sang until it was safely across. The boats on the river fired guns, had crews stand at attention, sounded whistles, and flew flags at half-mast.

At 10:00 A.M., the ferry with the funeral car reached the Debrosses Street ferry landing. The casket was immediately seated in an elaborate, plumed hearse on a platform five feet off the ground so people in the distance could see it.

The units making up the procession were in place. Escorted by the 7th Regiment of the New York National Guard, they began their solemn march up Hudson Street, then over to Canal Street, and finally down Broadway to city hall. It was a huge affair. The sound of horses' hooves and boots on the street together with the glinting of drawn sabers and tall flags was stirring.

As many as one hundred twenty-five thousand viewed the president's remains. Once again, German musical societies with a thousand combined voices sang mournful requiems nearby as the viewing went on day and night. General Townsend, the commander of the train, hoped the German choir was keeping New Yorkers sedate. A string of violent uprisings, the latest being the Draft Riots, convinced him these people welcomed situations that caused them to stir things up. He hoped with all his heart that everything went off without incident.

There was one issue with the potential to ignite unrest—the initial refusal of New York's city council to allow black marchers in the procession. "No Negroes Marching!" was the terse order from the aldermen. An editorial in the *New York Evening Post*, detailed in *The Best American History Essays on Lincoln*, edited by Sean Wilentz, didn't pull its punches in its reaction: "Our late President was venerated by the whole colored population with a peculiar degree of feeling, and they looked upon him as the liberator of their race. We have accepted the services of colored citizens in the war and it is disgraceful ingratitude to shut them out of our civil demonstrations."

Stanton, when apprised of this, responded angrily in a telegram to the New York City Council: "It is the desire of the Secretary of War that no discrimination respecting color should be exercised in admitting persons to the funeral procession tomorrow. In this city [Washington] a black regiment formed part of the escort."

Meanwhile, the president's body was starting to visibly decay. He'd been dead almost ten days. The *New York Times* of April 25, 1865, hinted at this, staying within the lines of good taste:

> Hastily and reverently, the people approached, and with uncovered head, bent forward to seize an impression of the honored features. To those who had not seen Mr. Lincoln in life, the view may be satisfactory, but to those who were familiar with his features, it is far otherwise. The color is leaden, almost brown; the forehead recedes sharp and clearly marked; the eyes deep sunk and close held upon the sockets; the cheek bones, always high are unusually prominent; the cheeks hollowed and deep pitted; the unnaturally thin lips shut tight and firm as if glued together; and the small chin, covered with slight beard, seemed pointed and sharp.

At city hall, two photos of the corpse were taken. One survived, having been kept in Stanton's files. He was furious when he learned that General Townsend authorized the photographs. He immediately telegraphed and upbraided him, demanding that he confiscate the glass negatives and all prints. Up until then, the commander had been sending Stanton glowing appraisals of the trip. He even said Lincoln's body was holding up when others said it was decomposing. He was stricken by Stanton's harshness. The secretary was a deadly serious man with a wicked temper. Townsend immediately confiscated the negatives and prints per Stanton's orders.

The casket was closed at 11:00 A.M., Tuesday, April 25. Carried from city hall to the hearse, it was then drawn by sixteen white horses, each lead by a groom. The procession arrived at the Hudson River Railroad station at Thirtieth Street at 12:30 P.M. An estimated five hundred thousand participated in the New York City obsequies.

The pilot train, drawn by the locomotive Constitution, departed the station at 4:15 P.M. Ten minutes later, the locomotive Union chugged out with the funeral train. Engineer William Buchanan brought it evenly north along the Hudson River. There was no regret in Townsend's heart as the New York City skyline diminished outside the window of the officers car. The mishap with the photos had left him rattled.

The funeral train hugged the east bank of the Hudson, hitting one small town after another on its journey to Albany: Fort Washington, Mount Saint Vincent, Yonkers, Hastings, Dobbs Ferry, Irvington, Tarrytown, Ossining, Montrose, and Peekskill. A stop was made at Garrison's Landing at 6:20 P.M. West Point loomed dull and fortresslike high in the hills across the river. The entire corps of cadets had crossed the river and stood at attention as the train rolled to a stop at the landing. They were then given the honor of passing through the funeral car to pay their respects. At Poughkeepsie, thousands huddled at the small hilltop depot. They watched a prominent local citizen, Mathew Vassar, board the funeral car to rest a wreath of magnolia blossoms, plucked from his own tree, on the casket. It was considered one of the more touching moments of the entire funeral.

The Union's drive rods and pistons were oiled. The sand dome was filled. The woodpile was topped off, and the tender's water tank refilled. When the steam gauge on the backhead showed sufficient pressure, the tender's brakes were released. (Most locos didn't have brakes because they tended to knock the wheels out of alignment, or quarter.) The throttle was eased forward. The fireman tugged the cord attached to the bell, and the clapper clanged it loudly.

Leaning out the cab window, the engineer watched for the signal from the switchman's lantern. Crewmen at the station nervously checked their pocket watches. It was important that everyone was in sync. Because there was no universal time source—such as today's atomic clocks—there could be time variations of up to fifteen minutes between cities and towns. Fortunately the Hudson River Railroad standardized everything: the track gauge, dispatching procedures, and time itself. In those days, railroads could dictate time along their lines. Most crewmen used high-quality, seventeen-jewel pocket watches that were regularly cleaned and adjusted by the railroad's jewelers.

When the switchman wagged his lantern, giving the "all clear," the engineer pushed the throttle. A few quick whistle blasts and the train rolled away, chuffing into the moist spring twilight.

The journey took it through the wealthy communities of Hyde Park, Staatsburg, Rhinebeck, Barrytown, Tivoli, Germantown, and Catskill.

The Catskill Mountains had sunk into a line of brooding shadows when the train reached the town of Hudson at 9:45 P.M. Thousands waited to say farewell to the commander in chief. It was then on to Stockport, Stuyvesant, and Castleton.

At 10:55 it rolled into East Albany. Under the illumination of many torches, soldiers and firemen from three companies carefully guided the funeral party and casket across the Hudson River and into Albany. Pallbearers then carried the casket to a catafalque in the Assembly Chamber of the state Capitol.

Four days before the arrival of the train, the legislature finally voted to ratify the Thirteenth Amendment. The opposition was sensitive to how bad it would look if it received the Great Emancipator without having ratified emancipation. Calvert Comstock, an adviser to the Democrats in the New York State Legislature, told them, "Let us refuse to ever seem in a disloyal position or as the defenders of Slavery." This speaks to the accepted notion that all Northerners opposed slavery.

Albany's funeral sendoff, the first west of the Hudson, was simpler than those down the line. Although restrained, it was still impressive and occasionally bold. The city was shrouded in black mourning. Touching statements were draped across buildings:

"Though dead, he still speaketh."

"The great heart of the nation throbs heavily at the portals of the grave."

"And the mourners go about the streets."

"And the victory that day was turned into mourning unto all the people."

Some of the more touching sentiments were Lincoln quotes:

"The heart of the nation throbs heavily at the portraits of the tomb."

"Let us resolve that the martyred dead shall not have died in vain."

At 2:00 P.M., after viewing ended, a procession watched six white horses pull the hearse down Broadway to the train station. Four bands were included in the escort, and they played at various times "Auld Lang Syne," "Love Not," and "Come and Let Us Worship." Telegraph lines across the country were bristling with the news that John Wilkes Booth had been killed. At 4:00 P.M., the funeral train pulled out of the Albany station amid the tolling of bells.

Responsibility for the train now fell to the New York Central Railroad. The locomotive Dean Richmond was polished and fueled. The hand railings along the boiler were wrapped with strands of bunting, the cab windows had black mourning cloth along their tops, and American flags fluttered from stands on the coupler brace. The train lunged into the heart of abolitionist country, home to Sojourner Truth, Frederick Douglass, Susan B. Anthony, Elizabeth Cady Stanton, and Obadiah Bush, who had died in 1851. A forebearer of the Bush presidents, Obadiah was once vice president of the Anti-Slavery Society. Deeply involved with the Underground Railroad, he called for New York to secede from the Union because of slavery. New York began legislating abolition as early as 1781 but didn't achieve full enactment until 1827. This tells us how long regional fracturing over slavery extended.

The Dean Richmond, with engineer George W. Wrightson at the throttle, took the train with its three coaches, three sleepers, funeral car, and officers car steadily west through upstate New York. It hit Schenectady, then Amsterdam, Fonda, Palatine Bridge, Rome, Green's Corner, Verona, Oneida, Canastota, Chittenango, Kirkville, and Manlius. At Syracuse, thirty-five thousand greeted the train during its brief 11:15 P.M. stop. The station had enormous flags on both sides. Inside, illumination was added with four locomotive lanterns. Four more were placed outside on the platform. Evergreen trees were placed every ten feet along both sides of the station. Such was the excitement that authorities had trouble keeping people off the tracks.

Around midnight, the train rumbled to life, the slack of the couplers thumping as the train began to stretch forward. Continuing down the line until 3:00 A.M., it passed through Memphis, Jordan, Weedsport, Port Byron, Savannah, Clyde, Lyons, Newark, Palmyra, Macedon, and then Fairport. At each stop there were citizens waiting; sad, tired folks, most wanting to say they participated in the event.

At 3:20 A.M., on Thursday, April 27, the train rolled to a stop at the New York Central's Mill Street Station in Rochester. The station was situated in the city's industrial hub. Enormous stone mills and factories loomed over the Genesee River gorge. The mayor, twenty-five city council members, and civil groups shivered in the night air. Soldiers stood in a solemn line along the north side of the station. The massive train shed backed up to the Genesee River, the tracks running through the structure and then over a bridge spanning a spectacular waterfall. The falls powered the factories and mills via a raceway. Thickened by spring freshets, the falls bellowed in the stone amphitheater it plunged into. Church bells announced to the city that the train had arrived, echoing dully off the stone mills around the station.

Lincoln had stopped at this station during his inaugural train ride. He was to give a speech from the balcony of the adjacent Savoy Hotel—where you could get a plate of oysters and a glass of milk for twenty-five cents! The train was behind schedule, and the new president was exhausted, so instead he spoke briefly from his car platform.

Rochester had always been an antislavery hotbed. Frederick Douglass published his *North Star* antislavery newspaper up until 1851 just a few blocks south of the station. Susan B. Anthony lived a few blocks west, on Madison Street. The city was a primary stop on the Underground Railroad. The Genesee River was a mecca for runaway slaves. If they could reach its port on Lake Ontario, they could then sail to freedom in Canada. Indeed, the grief was real and deep among these heartbroken citizens, huddled to bid their Great Emancipator farewell. Even along the nearby Erie Canal, banners and wreaths hung from canal bridges, and canal packets were decorated with strands of black crepe.

It was reported that former president Millard Fillmore was in Rochester at the time and boarded the funeral train here and not in Batavia. Amid salutes from the 54th New York Infantry Regiment and the echoing blasts from a small battery, the train rolled out, passing on through Cold Water, Chili, Churchville, Bergen, Byron, Batavia, Crofts, Corfu, Alden, Wende, and Lancaster.

It had been a long night for the passengers. Jostled probably as far back as Amsterdam in sleeper-car bunks and convertible beds, they stepped off the train wobbly when it stopped in Buffalo at 8:00 A.M. Quite hungry, they managed to feign solemnity, standing with stiff formality and pretending not to be annoyed at the frantic cannon blasts alerting the city that Lincoln had arrived. They were then escorted to Bloomer's dining saloon for breakfast.

Buffalo was not altogether certain the train would have an extended stop, but it made plans just the same. Like many other cities and towns, Buffalo had already put on a large affair when Washington held its funeral procession and service on April 19.

After pallbearers carefully placed the casket in the hearse, Fillmore headed a procession through downtown Buffalo to Saint James Hall. In the photos taken that gray, gloomy morning, there is something biblical about the way the dark press of humanity followed the hearse, like the throngs that followed Jesus to his Crucifixion. In the crowd were many Canadians who came across the border to pay their respects.

Prior to the public viewing in Buffalo, the undertaker informed members of the press that it had been erroneously reported in newspapers that Lincoln's brain had been removed. Only a portion of the brain had been removed for the autopsy, after which it had been put back into the skull. It was also noted that there hadn't been any noticeable changes in Lincoln's face since leaving Washington, and that included its color. Other reports specifically mentioned the dark brown color of the face. Some of today's head trauma experts think the darkness was caused by blood filling the face at the time of the shooting. Embalming techniques of that day probably couldn't get all of it to drain out.

After the public viewing at Saint James Hall, the casket was returned to the Exchange Street station for 10:00 P.M. departure. A vivid description of the train was given in the April 29 issue of the *Buffalo Daily Courier*:

> Our space yesterday morning did not permit us to speak of the train which conveyed the remains of President Lincoln and the Guard of Honor from this city to Cleveland, and which was employed last night to bear them to Columbus. The pilot engine was the "Comet," Mr. Gus Catlin, engineer, and was under the immediate charge of Assistant Superintendent Williams. It was handsomely decorated with flags, flowers and tastefully draped with white and black crepe.
>
> The [funeral] train engine was the "Atlas," in charge of Mr. John Hart, one of the most accomplished engineers in the country. It was handsomely trimmed with flags, and crepe in festoons, and adorned with bouquets. The interior of the cab was concealed from outside by a monster American flag, and the light shining through it produced a fine effect. The cars, one of them a new and splendid sleeping car put upon the road for the first time, were decorated in exceeding good taste. The outside was draped with deep festoons of black apalachee, trimmed with silver braids and looped up with beautiful rosettes, which were fastened with silvered metal stars. The festoons on the inside were of lighter character, and swept gracefully from the

raised roofs to the sides of the cars. The baggage car had two monster stars in cloth on either side, in the center of which were black and white rosettes fastened with silvered metal stars.

The train skirted the shores of Lake Erie. The *Buffalo Daily Courier* described the scene at Dunkirk:

> The most elaborate demonstration on the line of the road, as the train passed along, was that made at Dunkirk. The depot was lighted in a brilliant manner and on a platform were thirty-six young ladies dressed in white, wearing black sashes and bearing banners in their hands, as they knelt.

The thirty-six young ladies represented the number of states at the end of the war. There were thirty-four when the war started. West Virginia was added in 1863, and Nevada in 1864. West Virginia was the first state to secede from the world's newest—though short-lived—nation, the Confederate States of America.

From Dunkirk, the train continued to Brocton and Westfield, where little Grace Bedell had told Lincoln on his inaugural stop that he should grow a beard. He took her advice.

The train again passed into Pennsylvania and stopped in Erie, where there was some confusion as to whether the train would stop or not. As a result, there was a poor showing at the station. After refueling, it was switched to another railroad and headed to points west.

Lincoln's private car sees the light of day, emerging from the Orange & Alexandria Railroad car shops at Alexandria, Virginia, to have its builder's portrait taken. It is a myth that Lincoln disapproved of its building, saying it was too pretentious at a time of war. Another myth is that he never rode it when alive. He gave it a test ride and was delighted with its performance. The car shares billing with the W. H. Whiton, a 4-4-0 built by Mason Locomotive Works and commissioned by the US Military Railroad. (*Library of Congress*)

Christened the United States, the car was intended as Lincoln's mobile headquarters. Believed to have been painted a deep maroon and highlighted with delicate, hand-painted striping, it was stunning. Modeled after the Pennsylvania Railroad's most elaborate passenger cars, this hybrid featured etched-glass windows, silver-plated appointments, and elaborate iron railings. (*Library of Congress*)

Some of the castings for the trucks were made from burst Civil War cannon. The unusual broad-tread wheels had 33-inch diameters. Intended to compensate for slight variances in railroad gauges, they tended to make the car slide from side to side, creating an unstable ride. The impressive harp-shaped guides featured patriotic flourishes and were painted red, white, and blue. Left of center above the truck are two large brass caps covering the bolster bolts.

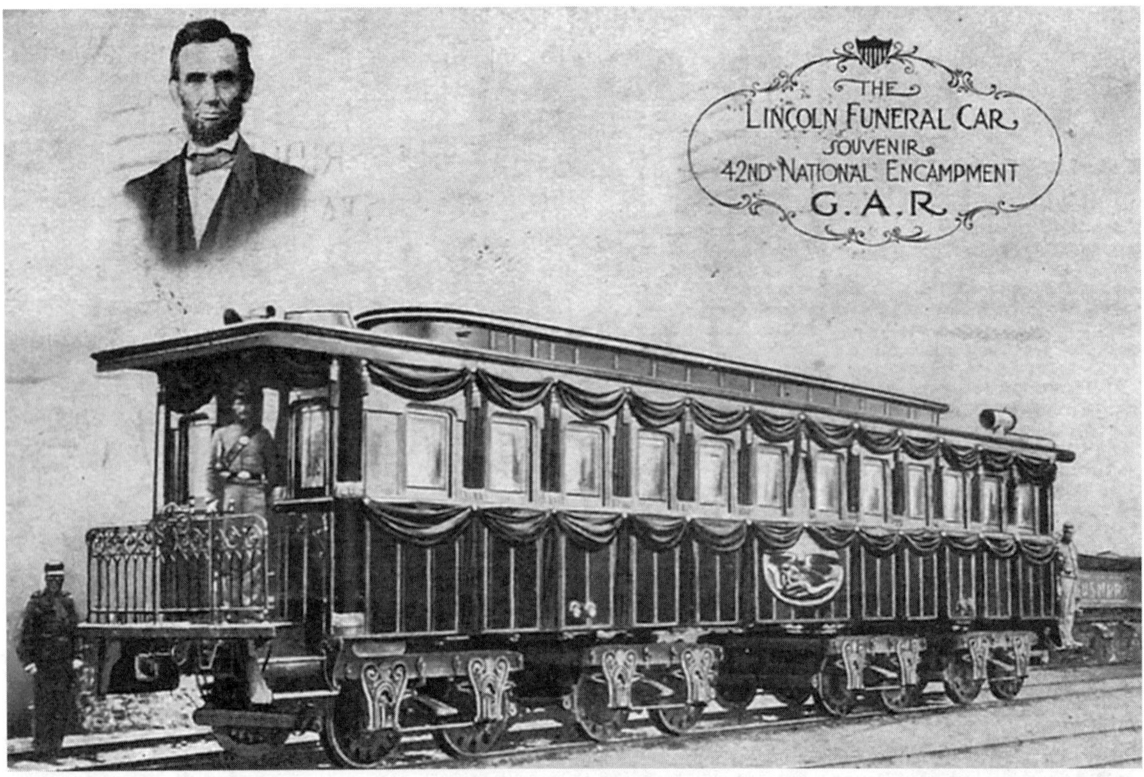

The United States, decorated and altered to accept Lincoln's casket. On the platform is Myron Hawley Lamson, superintendent of all car work on the US Military Railroad in Virginia. His involvement with the car was personal. He helped design and build it, and later he built the stand upon which the casket rested. As a member of the sergeant guard, he faithfully attended the car throughout the journey. (*Author's collection*)

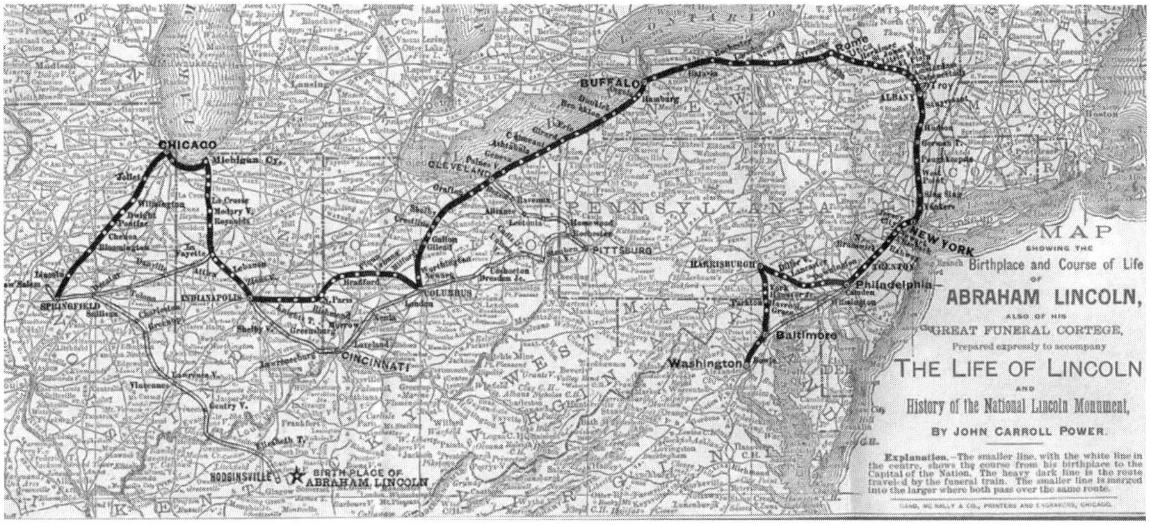

The route of the funeral train, designated the Lincoln Special, essentially retraced the approximately 1,650-mile journey of the president's inaugural train. (*Author's collection*)

A rendering of the car interior shows the casket and the ever-present guard of honor. The casket holding the remains of the president's son Willie was at the front of the car. (*Library of Congress*)

This Duncan Phyfe table (ca. 1850) was lent by the Pennsylvania Railroad to the government for use in the funeral. It was said to have supported Lincoln's casket, but a special, tapered stand was built specifically for that. Witnesses attested the table was in the car. It probably supported Willie's casket. On the return trip to Washington, some soldiers, released from the stress of the funeral, got drunk. A fight broke out in which one of table legs was broken. It was repaired in a Pennsylvania Railroad car shop. (*Author's collection*)

The 100-foot–tall, four-sided clock tower of Washington's Baltimore & Ohio (B&O) station is highlighted just beyond the left front corner in this 1861 image taken atop a wing of the Capitol. Lincoln arrived at the station incognito on February 22, 1861, to take the oath of office. The station (ca. 1851) handled over one hundred fifty thousand passengers a year. The image provides an interesting Civil War-era cityscape of the nation's seat of power. (*Library of Congress*)

The first leg of the Lincoln Special departed Washington's B&O station on April 21, 1865. The station is to the left in this postwar image. It stood on New Jersey Avenue. Willie's casket, taken from Oak Hill Cemetery in Georgetown, was already at the station when a somber procession from the Capitol brought his father's remains. The train, pulled by B&O locomotive no. 238, steamed out at 8:00 a.m. A pilot train, consisting of a locomotive and one passenger car, preceded the train by ten minutes to make sure the track, especially at crossings, was clear. (*Library of Congress*)

Lincoln's son Robert rode the thirty-eight miles to Baltimore but then returned to Washington to be with his mother, who refused to make the train ride at all. The B&O Camden station in Baltimore was built in the Italianate style from 1856 to 1867. A stop on the inaugural train, Lincoln would also use it on November 18, 1863, while en route to give his Gettysburg Address. The station welcomed the funeral train at 10:00 A.M., Friday, April 21. A procession brought the casket to the Merchant's Exchange Building for public viewing. This photo is dated 1865. (*Author's collection*)

Far beyond the lavish pageantry of the funeral, more modest farewells were made. A Union soldier grieves over the grave of a fallen friend in a hastily built cemetery at Richmond, Virginia. The war was over and many Union troop were leaving the fallen capital. (*Library of Congress*)

After the public viewing in Baltimore, the casket was brought to the Northern Central Railroad's Calvert Street station, pictured in this Civil War-era photo. Reports indicate the funeral car and officers car were towed to the station by mules along a street railroad, of which there were many in those days. The train departed for Harrisburg, Pennsylvania, at 3:00 P.M. (*Author's collection*)

Military installations such as Fort Whipple at Arlington, Virginia, displayed appropriate symbols of grieving, as evidenced by the black cloth draped above the door and windows. Part of a network of fortifications constructed to defend Washington during the war, the fort was named after Brevet Major General Amiel Week Whipple, who died in service in May 1863. Seated in the folding camp chair to the left is a Captain Nevins, flanked by several officers. (*Library of Congress*)

This November 1863 image at Hanover Junction, Pennsylvania, shows a special train and dignitaries en route to the dedication of the cemetery at Gettysburg. Lincoln stopped here at the same time. The funeral train would make a fueling stop here. (*Library of Congress*)

The train during its stay at Harrisburg, Pennsylvania. Guards were posted at both ends of the car when it was parked. (*Author's collection*)

Another view at Harrisburg. The train was pulled by Pennsylvania Railroad locomotive no. 331. (*Author's collection*)

A single length of black bunting draped over the door expresses the sadness felt at this federal field hospital structure in York, Pennsylvania. The structure was part of a huge field hospital established in Penn Common, a public meeting area dating back to York's founding in 1741. Of the slightly more than fourteen thousand sick and wounded cared for there during the Civil War, only 193 died. It was a remarkable survival and recovery rate. The hospital's brass band played for the crowd when Lincoln's funeral train arrived. (*Author's collection*)

Pennsylvania Railroad locomotive no. 331 is festooned with flags as it arrives at the Philadelphia, Wilmington, and Baltimore Railroad station in West Philadelphia on April 22, 1865. It arrived amid the booming of cannons, church bells tolling, and volunteer bands playing. This is one of few photos showing the entire train. The last car is the officers car. The United States is next. Crewmen and officials pose beside the locomotive. The engineer, John Miller, is at the front holding an oilcan. The president's casket was transported from here to the Kensington Street station after public viewing. (*Author's collection*)

Locomotive no. 331 with the funeral car and the officers car in West Philadelphia. As the president lay in state at Independence Hall, the train was moved to the Kensington Street station and prepared for departure the following day, April 24, at 4:00 A.M. (*Author's collection*)

In this view of no. 331, the crew takes time for a photo while gathered on the tender. Beside the locomotive is a sleeper car. Rarely photographed, these lavish cars could cost up to $20,000—as much as a locomotive and tender. A lavish Pullman sleeper was added to the funeral train during its last leg to Springfield. (*Author's collection*)

All businesses were closed in Philadelphia while the president lay in state at Independence Hall. Downtown was seemingly filled with the entire population of the city. Bedlam broke out when angry citizens were forced to wait in a three-mile-long line while more prominent citizens were given preferred viewing of the casket. In this stereoview, a police line is trying to hold back the anxious back. (*Library of Congress*)

The hearse parked on a cobblestone street near Independence Hall. (*Author's collection*)

Mourners swarmed the streets of Philadelphia, desperate to glimpse the hearse and casket. Eleven divisions of soldiers and several bands accompanied the procession. The clamor of cannon and church bells made the event more stirring. At times the streets were so clogged with onlookers that the procession was halted. (*Author's collection*)

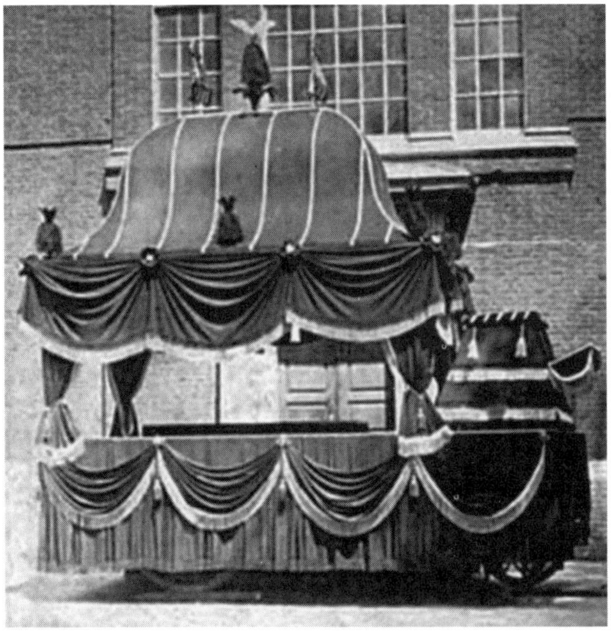

The elaborate hearse, adorned with silver fittings and black fringe, glimmers in the sun-filled Saturday that it carried the casket to Independence Hall. There were two days of viewing in Philadelphia. (*Author's collection*)

On the lawn of Independence Hall, processional crowds await the arrival of the casket. (*Author's collection*)

Ulysses S. Grant and his wife's Philadelphia home is wonderfully decorated during the event. (*Author's collection*)

Part of the Philadelphia cortege. (*Author's collection*)

Commercial buildings on New York City's Broadway are being decorated in anticipation of the funeral. (*Library of Congress*)

After arriving at Jersey City, New Jersey, left, the funeral car was transported across the Hudson River to the Debrosses Street ferry landing in Manhattan. This is a view of the Jersey City Ferry landing at the end of Courtland Street. An illustration, right, of the barge, or steam lighter, transporting the funeral car from the New Jersey side of the Hudson to Manhattan. The illustration shows raised flags, but most vessels on the river lowered theirs to half-mast. They also paid respects with whistle blasts and gunshots. (*Author's collection*)

The United States rail car has arrived at Manhattan's Debrosses Street ferry, and the casket has been placed in the hearse. The procession is about to commence. (*Author's collection*)

In one of clearest stereoviews of the entire funeral, Lincoln's casket is visible in the hearse during the New York City obsequies. (*Author's collection*)

The New York funeral was the most ambitious event the city ever hosted. As word of it spread to cities up the train route, some funeral committees felt a need to upstage it. (*Author's collection*)

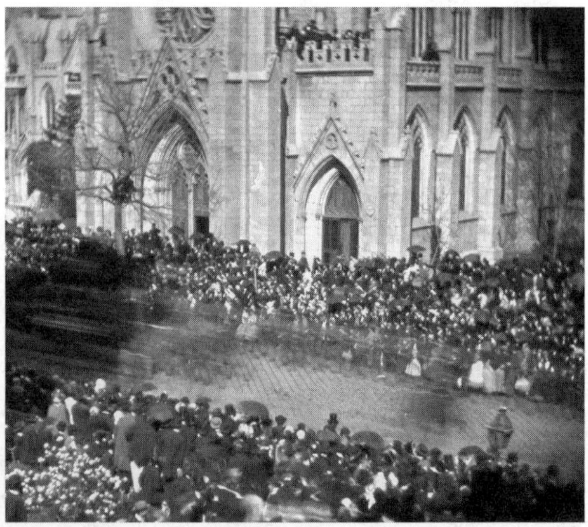

These two images are excerpted from a negative exposed in a four lens stereo camera. The exposures were taken April 25 from a window at Mathew Brady's New York City studio, across the street from Grace Church. The procession with the hearse, blurred in the second image, was moving up Broadway, having just come from city hall, where the casket was on public display. Onlookers can be seen in the tree and on church balconies. (*National Archives*)

A close-up view of the hearse used in New York. (*Library of Congress*)

New York City Hall is adorned in bunting and crepe. Mourners ascend the steps to view the remains placed in the rotunda. An estimated one hundred twenty-five thousand people filed past the open casket. (*Author's collection*)

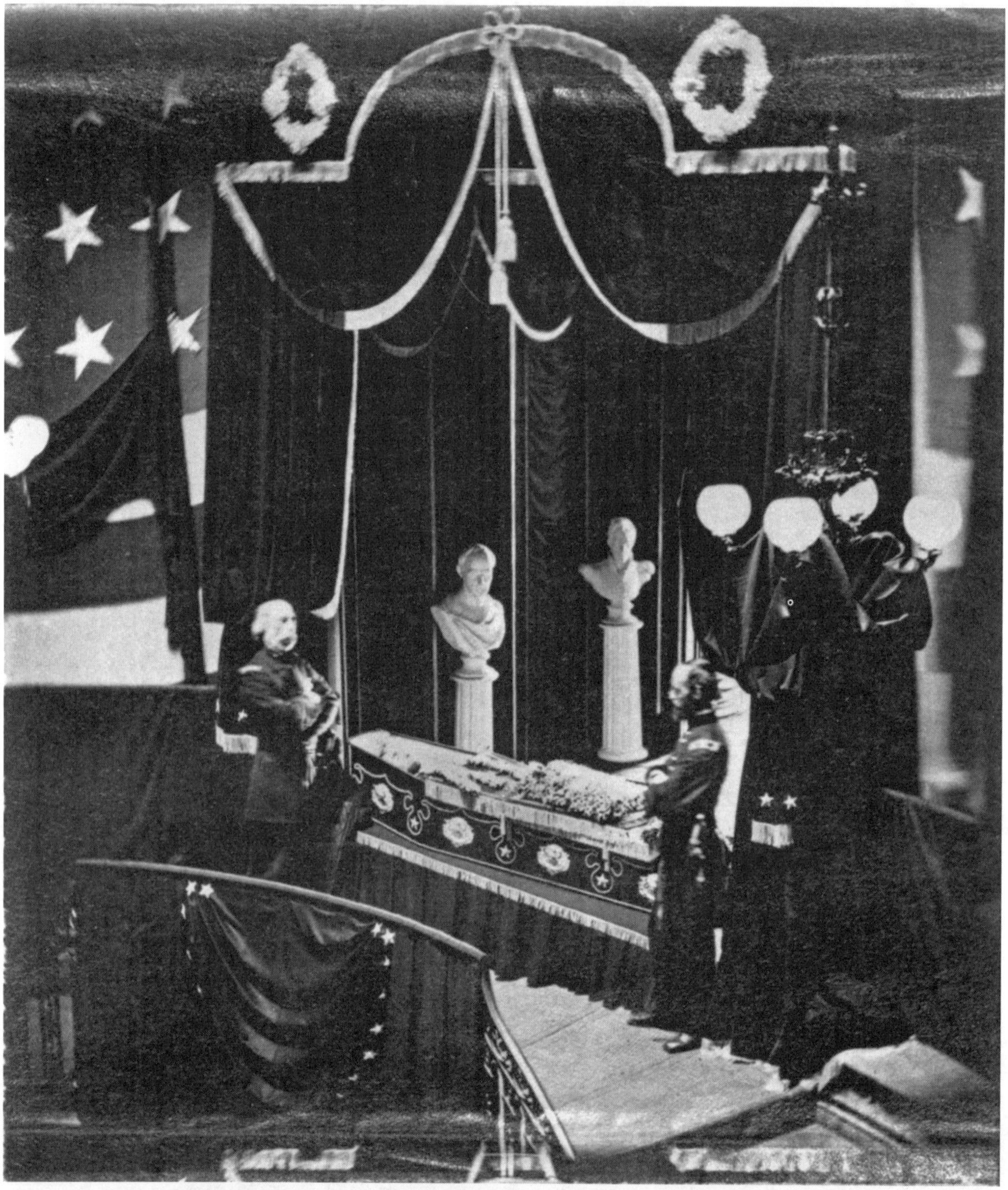

Secretary of War Edwin M. Stanton forbade that any photos be taken of Lincoln's corpse. This one taken in New York survived and was kept by Stanton himself. (*Author's collection*)

One of the more unusual images shows the procession moving past the Cornelius van Schaak Roosevelt mansion (square building on left) on New York's Broadway. Cornelius was Teddy Roosevelt's grandfather. In the second-story window is the future president, Teddy, as a boy. The image is unique for the period in that it contains two presidents. A close-up of this strange historical coincidence shows young Teddy in the window with his brother Elliott, future father of Eleanor Roosevelt. Also in the house was Edith Carow, who became Teddy's second wife and first lady. She commented about the funeral, "I was a little girl and my governess took me to Grandfather Roosevelt's house on Broadway so I could watch the funeral procession. But as I looked down from the window and saw all the black drapings, I became frightened and started to cry." The two boys, annoyed at her crying, "locked me in a back room. I never did get to see the funeral." (*Library of Congress*)

Military units move up Broadway. There are men in the tree and even on rooftops. Prime viewing spots could be expensive: homeowners and merchants along the procession routes rented spots at their windows for over one hundred dollars. (*Library of Congress*)

A bird's-eye view of the New York procession. (*Library of Congress*)

A rendering of the funeral train leaving New York's Hudson River Railroad station on Thirtieth Street. A major part of the hysteria of the funeral centered on seeing the train, fantastic in its elaborate mourning decorations. People came to see it as much as the dead president. (*Author's collection*)

A twentieth-century view of New York's Thirtieth Street railroad station. Lincoln was the first passenger to use the station when his inaugural train left here in 1860 for Washington. The station, left, was demolished in the 1930s. (*Author's collection*)

Nearly all of the locomotives participating in the funeral are recorded in history. This touched-up photo may be the only one of the famous Union, all decked out for the funeral. The Hudson River Railroad 4-4-0 departed the Thirtieth Street station pulling the nine-car funeral train. The pilot train, pulled by the Constitution, preceded it by ten minutes. The trains made many stops before arriving in Albany.
(*Author's collection*)

Dutifully pulling its special train north along the west side of the Hudson River, the Union made stops every twenty miles or so for fueling. At Ossining, New York, the train passed under this substantial memorial arch in the vicinity of Sing Sing Prison. The fortresslike stone prison opened in 1826. *Sing Sing* is derived from the Indian *snick snick*, meaning stone upon stone. Numerous funeral—or memorial—arches were built over the tracks along the journey.
(*Author's collection*)

The citizens of Yonkers, New York, honored the late president with a funeral arch in town. Many such arches appeared around the country, some simple and thoughtful, others grand and ambitious. These temporary arches were often fretted with vines, pine bows, and flowers. They were intended for memorial and remembrance.
(*Author's collection*)

Chuffing north in New York, the Union stopped at some of the smallest towns along the entire route, Cold Spring being an example. The large structure is the Cold Spring station, with the tracks visible in front. (*Author's collection*)

The train arrived at Albany on April 25. A huge procession led the hearse from the train station to city hall. The long exposure made a streaky blur of the cortege. An estimated fifty thousand citizens filled the city's black-draped downtown. (*Author's collection*)

Albany put on a memorable farewell. This view shows the procession (blurred by a long exposure) on its way to city hall, where the casket was opened for public viewing. New York secretary of state Chauncey M. Depew described the president lying in state: "The face had an expression of absolute content, of relief, at throwing off a burden such as few men have been called upon to bear—a burden which few could have borne." (*Author's collection*)

A close-up image of the crowd and decorations on State Street along the procession route in Albany. (*Author's collection*)

The hearse with six white horses waits outside Albany City Hall at Eagle and Washington streets. The doors were opened at 1:15 A.M. and remained open more than twelve hours to accommodate the tens of thousands who came to pay their respects. Approximately four thousand passed the casket each hour. When the doors were closed at 1:30 P.M., thousands were still waiting in a line nearly a mile long. (*Author's collection*)

New York Central's locomotive Dean Richmond assumed responsibility for the train from Albany, New York, to Erie, Pennsylvania. (*Author's collection*)

The train stopped at this station in Troy, New York, pictured in a postwar image. (*Author's collection*)

The Lincoln Special rolled into Utica, New York, at 8:25 P.M., Wednesday, April 26. The station is to the right in this postwar image. (*Author's collection*)

A stop was made at Auburn's New York Central station, visible on the left. A primitive pioneer style loco from the 1840s is performing yard service. (*Author's collection*)

The through station (ca. 1839) in Syracuse, New York's Vanderbilt Square was a stop for both the inaugural and funeral trains. In the early days, a bell atop the station would announce the arrival of trains. The station was demolished in 1869. The funeral train, arriving at 11:15 P.M., April 25, was met by a crowd of heartbroken citizens. It departed fifteen minutes later. (*Author's collection*)

Rochester's New York Central Station as it appeared in the Civil War era. Lincoln was supposed to give a short address from the balcony of the Savoy Hotel balcony (right), but his inaugural train was off schedule. Instead, he spoke briefly from the back of the car. Upstate New York was the cradle of the abolitionist movement. Rochester was home to Frederick Douglass and Susan B. Anthony as well as being a major stop on the Underground Railroad. A loyal crowd waited as the funeral train pulled in around 3:20 A.M. They bade a quiet and heartfelt farewell to their Great Emancipator. (*Author's collection*)

The citizens of Batavia, New York, were determined to project their grief and outrage over the murder by extensively decorating their humble Union Station. This is one of the only photos showing mourners gathered at a station. (*Author's collection*)

The train rolled into Buffalo at 7:00 A.M., April 27. This is a postwar view of the New York Central's Exchange Street station. It had been suitably decorated, as were most buildings in the vicinity. Throngs gathered by the station in the predawn hours in anticipation of the train's arrival.
(*Author's collection*)

April 27 was a cloudy, dismal day when thousands filled Buffalo's Main Street to watch the funeral procession. (*Author's collection*)

The press of anguished mourners watching the hearse wobble up Main Street was a scene repeated in many cities. Some likened it to the crowd following Christ to his Crucifixion. In the mania caused by the funeral, Lincoln underwent an apotheosis—a transformation from human to divine status. He was elevated to America's saint. (*Author's collection*)

This view of Buffalo's procession was taken from the window of Pond & Hambleton's Photograph Gallery on the west side of Main Street. The hearse had a formidable military escort. Onlookers watch from the rooftops and windows of commercial buildings. (*Author's collection*)

A superlative rendering of the hearse and six horses used in Buffalo. The hearse was built by Buffalo carriage builders Cheesman and Dodge. The six white horses with black blankets were tended by African American grooms. (*Author's collection*)

From Buffalo, the train headed for Cleveland, lunging briefly into Pennsylvania, where it stopped at the Erie Union Depot, pictured in this Civil War-era image. Construction of the Italianate depot, which served four railroads, was nearly complete when the train arrived at 2:50 A.M., April 28. (*Author's collection*)

THREE

"THE MIRTH OF THE LAND IS GONE"

As accounts of the fantastic funeral pageant were telegraphed not just up the train's route but also across the country, an almost frenzied need to somehow be personally involved in it persisted. Families made long, grueling rides to see the train. Specially formed trains were quickly dispatched to bring dignitaries to major cities. There didn't seem to be a break in the rows of mourners lining both sides of the track. Houses and businesses within eyeshot of the tracks put up signs and flower-bedecked memorials for the passengers to see.

Fights broke out within the dense crowds as tempers wore thin. Businesses that didn't close during the train's visit got bricks thrown through their windows, or their employees were harassed. Negative editorials were met with hostility. There were reports that people were killed during the twenty-day event. With businesses closed, people had to deal with hunger and thirst during their long hours of waiting. Shop owners lost revenue. We are left to wonder how the massive sanitation concerns were dealt with because no records have been found on the matter.

Funeral committees in towns and cities slated for stops bickered among themselves as they scrutinized newspaper accounts, frantically seeking theatrics to make their experience showier. Budgets were busted and debts run up as additional supplies were demanded. An insatiable need for any kind of black fabric or patriotic bunting developed. There was price gouging for wood, nails, string, paper, and paint—anything that could be used in a display. A market for postmortem art inspired by Lincoln's death sprang up.

Through it all, Americans were physically and emotionally overwhelmed. They were tired from long hours of preparing ceremonies and waiting in lines. Some waited days on lawns outside civic buildings where the president's corpse was to be displayed. Daily schedules were thrown off. Kids were cranky.

Yet there was something thrilling about the whole affair. There was an exhilarating madness to it and a sense they were emerging as a new people. The war had been devastating. New depths of national and personal grief had been plumbed, and that was before this latest tragedy. Now a new layer of suffering had to be experienced.

There was a maelstrom of social change at a time when people wanted to settle back into prewar stability. It was bewildering and disconcerting. Invisible forces were at work. The psychological wreckage of the war was fast upon everyone. The monumental and appalling grief over lost brothers, husbands, and sons was fresh and stabbing. Thousands of newly orphaned children were gathering into savage little bands that robbed and harassed. Women didn't have jobs as they do today. Without their husbands' incomes, they couldn't afford to raise their children. In many cases the offspring were abandoned to the street. Veterans plagued with posttraumatic stress turned to drink and drugs, and they were usually institutionalized or condemned as weaklings. Perhaps as many as one hundred thousand died of their wounds in the first year following the war. Recent developments in genealogical research methods bear this out.

Additionally, America was easing away from its Victorian influences and questing toward its own identity. It had been a nation swirling in romanticism—a romanticism that collided with the startling reality of a brutal war. It was a wake-up call to be sure.

Furthermore, there was the emergence of vast new sociological and political concepts. Darwinism was gaining popularity. At worst it said there was no God. At best it suggested there might be a God but it could not directly influence our lives. There was the emergence of Marxism, with its convoluted quest for equality. Lincoln had received a letter from Karl Marx praising him for his abolition of slavery. Rambling and confused, it must have left Lincoln befuddled. It probably set off alarm bells. Marxism was antithetical to liberty.

Americans certainly had a lot on their plates. But they didn't shy away from any of it. America had become the test lab for numerous social awakenings that included civil rights, human rights, and women's rights.

As much as Lincoln championed personal liberty, his legacy is contested over what appear to be terrible violations of individual rights. His suspension of habeas corpus led to the imprisonment without trial of possibly ten thousand war protesters and suspected traitors. He shut down newspapers that editorially opposed him. Thousands of Southern civilians were killed by his brutal execution of the war, primarily through Sherman's devastating march and the ferocious shelling of cities.

Most of the South understandably hated him. Many found his murder providential, although Robert E Lee, Jefferson Davis, and other prominent citizens expressed regret over it. Lee provided a calming voice that quelled a possible resurgence of the cause after the murder.

John Wilkes Booth was exalted in some Southern circles. "All honor to J. Wilkes Booth," wrote Southern diarist Kate Stone. She lashed out wickedly against Lincoln and Seward. "What torrents of blood Lincoln has caused to flow, and how Secretary of State William Seward had aided him in his work. I cannot be sorry for their fate. They deserve it. They have reaped their just reward."

Of course, freed slaves despaired of Lincoln's death. They knew they had a friend in Lincoln. He would not have allowed the intolerable treatment they went on to receive at the hands of Southern aristocrats. Frederick Douglass lamented years after the death, "I assume had Lincoln been spared to see this day, the Negro of the South would have had more hope for enfranchisement."

In Charleston, South Carolina, former governor William Aiken gave a surprisingly moving address to the citizens of the city at Hibernian Hall. In an article published in the April 22 *New York Times*, it was clear he anguished over Lincoln's death:

> Fellow Citizens—We are assembled to pour out the general grief which has been felt in this city for the sudden removal from this life of Abraham Lincoln, late President of the United States. The horrible and atrocious assassination of President Lincoln has filled every feeling heart with sorrow and indignation. I did not know personally the late President, but those who did have spoken of him in the kindest manner to me; his heart was benevolent and forgiving, and we are told, and have reason to believe, that through him our difficulties would soon have been adjusted and peace once more restored to our distracted country. Our expressions of disgust for the dastardly wretch, who could have conceived and executed such a diabolical deed, can scarcely be uttered. Murder is always appalling, but more particularly so in this momentous crisis of our country—now our most anxious moment.
>
> Can it be believed that in the nineteenth century a human being could be found to have in his bosom so diabolical an idea, and with an accomplice enter the sick bedroom of another eminent and distinguished personage, the Secretary of State, and plunge into his bosom the deadly weapon? The heart sickens at the recital of such horrors.

Funeral sermons up North ranged from profound to ridiculous. Most rejected vengeance. Those in the South—given under the cautious eyes of their occupiers—generally expressed regret and even apprehension. Among the more ridiculous were those preaching that God punished America because it was, at heart, a wicked nation. Some espoused that God had Lincoln murdered in a theater to show the evils of theater going.

The train continued to steam out of moist, fragrant mornings and deep into the spring twilight. Engineer J. W. McGuire took the throttle at Erie, Pennsylvania, driving the William Case along the Cleveland, Painesville & Ashtabula Railroad. Departure from Erie was on Friday, April 28. Crossing the Ohio state line, the train passed through Conneaut, Kingsville, Ashtabula, Geneva, Madison, Perry, Painesville, Mentor, Willoughby, Wickliffe, and Euclid.

The train rolled valiantly along the lakeshore tracks and arrived at Cleveland's Union Station. Townsend telegraphed Washington that the train arrived safely at 6:50 A.M. on Friday, April 28. Thousands standing along the shore witnessed the regal entrance. A singularly bizarre display presented itself: a Miss Fields, a resident of nearby Wilson Street, erected a funeral arch from evergreens. When the train approached, she entered the arch dressed as the Goddess of Liberty in mourning.

An interesting account of decorating the pilot locomotive Dispatch was provided in a newspaper interview with Martin Fetter, then an employee at the rail yard. He was eighty-two when he gave the interview and mistakenly thought he had decorated the locomotive that pulled the funeral train. His account, found in the files of the Lincoln Financial Foundation Collection, may be the only one that relates what went into decorating any of the pilot engines. The use of the president's portrait in front of the engine must have made a deep impression on mourners:

> I was a lad then, not more than fifteen. When I reported for work I was surprised to find Engine #40, the "Dispatch," standing on a siding with a large crowd around her. I was gaping at the crowd when the boss came over and said: "That engine's going to pull President Lincoln's funeral train out of Cleveland and I'd like you to help trim her." . . . I started by shining up the brass around the cab. For a time I worked alone. Then the engineer, Bill Simmons, and the fireman, Joe Denslow, came over with the boss's daughter, Lavinia Hamm. They had white and black bunting and a large portrait of Lincoln in a gilt frame. I assisted Bill in putting up the picture right out in front of the engine, then we fastened several yards of bunting around it. Joe and Lavinia draped the sides. Before they got through, I climbed on top and muffled the bell. All in all it was a pretty job.

By odd coincidence, Fetter would help decorate the engine that pulled President James A. Garfield's funeral train sixteen years later.

The train did not remain long at Union Station. It was immediately run in reverse to the Euclid Avenue Station, arriving there twenty minutes later. A salute of thirty-six guns welcomed it.

There was no building in Cleveland large enough to handle the expected masses. Viewing would be at a beautiful pagoda built in Monument Square for this purpose. A procession brought the casket; prayers were said, and the viewing began. Mourners waited in the rain for their turn to enter. The compact and carpeted pagoda, or pavilion, as the Clevelanders referred to it, was a fanciful affair, perhaps a bit overdecorated, with golden eagles, immense plumes of black crepe, rosettes, streamers, and evergreen covered walls. And there were, of course, masses of flowers everywhere. The embalmer again prepared the body, as he did prior to every public showing, and viewing commenced.

At 10:00 P.M., the pagoda was closed after accommodating an estimated one hundred thousand citizens. The procession back to the depot passed large wreaths, shields, and crosses all skillfully decorated with flowers and now all rain soaked.

When the train departed at midnight, flowers were tossed onto the tracks ahead of it. Bill Simmons used the locomotive Dispatch to prepare the train for the next leg of the journey, leaving some cars behind and taking on new ones. The train was usually reconfigured at each major stop. The wonderfully decorated Nashville, with a portrait of Lincoln wired to the front, was being fired (a strong fire being built in its smoke box) during the return procession. Engineer James Gourley would handle the run to Columbus, Ohio.

The passengers prepared for sleep aboard the sturdy, elegant cars. In the sleepers, bunks were lowered and folding chairs were put on the floor so sofas and convertible seats could be formed into makeshift beds. The miserable rain continued, making the cars cold and damp. Outside, people stood in the rain, shivering beside the tracks in lines that stretched for miles.

The train continued to run slowly to allow long, lingering gazes. The Nashville's headlamp and signal lamps lit the gloomy faces ahead. The truth of the biblical text used in many of the funeral sermons, "The mirth of the land is gone" (Isaiah 24:11), was apparent. The funeral car was illuminated, the guards of honor and casket visible through the windows. That image had a way of burning itself into peoples' minds. There was even something solemn in the clicking of the wheels on the tracks.

The Lincoln Special steamed through Berea, Olmstead, Columbia, Grafton, La Grange, Wellington, Iberia, Cardington, Ashley, Eden, and Worthington, among other places. Thousands greeted the train at these places. The train didn't stop at all of them, but it did slow to a crawl—about five miles an hour—so a good look could be had. Crosses, messages of tribute, flowered shields, and a profusion of flags were attached to bridges.

Gliding in like a bejeweled empress, the Nashville slowed to a stop outside Columbus's Union Station at 7:30 A.M., Saturday, April 29. As the locomotive hissed and panted in front of the cavernous train shed, the casket was removed and placed in the hearse waiting across High Street. An escort of the 88th Ohio Volunteer Infantry led the procession to the Capitol. Soldiers marching on either side of the hearse had sabers drawn. Pallbearers brought the casket to the rotunda and set it on a low bier. It was covered in flowers, primarily lilacs, to help mask odors being generated by the corpse. People who passed the casket later associated the smell of lilacs with the experience in the rotunda. For some the scent of lilacs would bring on a depression. Others said the scent would make them gag.

Meanwhile, the manhunt for Jefferson Davis continued. He was moving deeper into the South with a stash of gold and silver from the Confederate Treasury. Honorable to the end, he would not use a penny of it to relieve his own harrowing financial circumstances.

The Confederacy continued to crumble around him, and he was finding himself less and less welcome in the land that once revered him. Having Union guerrillas bearing down on him may have added to the cold shoulder he was receiving. The South was a shambles, its conquered people fearful of retribution for Lincoln's murder.

The funeral train left Columbus at 8:00 P.M. Saturday, April 29, with the tolling of bells—an aspect of the national funeral that occurred along its entire route. The Nashville took it through Pleasant Valley, Unionville, Milford, Woodstock, Urbana, Covington, and New Paris. Somewhere during all this, a shadow train passed, apparently unnoticed. It was carrying Mary and her sons to Springfield.

The first stop in Indiana was Richmond. That was at 3:10 A.M. Sunday, April 30. A magnificent funeral arch, twenty-five-feet high and thirty-feet wide was erected over the tracks. Ten thousand to twelve thousand people waited at that early hour. The train stopped briefly outside the brooding, barrel-roofed train shed. All local engines were brought up and parked in the vicinity. Their headlamps were illuminated.

It was then on to places like Centerville, Cambridge City, Dublin, Lewisville, and others along the line. It arrived in Indianapolis at 8:00 A.M., April 30, at the Union Depot, and again it was raining. Sunday school children were the first allowed to view the president as he lay in state in the Capitol's rotunda. After them, a steady stream of mourners filed by. Shortly before midnight the doors were closed and the hearse returned the casket to the station.

The train left at 12:01 A.M., Monday, May 1, riding out on the Indianapolis & Lafayette Railroad and still drawn by the flashy Nashville. At 3:35 A.M. the train was moved over to the Louisville, New Albany & Chicago Railroad. The mechanics were always present during these maneuvers since there had been some difficulty getting the United States, with its peculiar, four-truck arrangement, through some stub switches.

At Lafayette, Indiana, the baton had been handed to engineer A. Rupert, who took the throttle of the Persian. The pilot train was pulled by the Rocket. After refueling, the Persian rolled slowly out on the Indianapolis & Lafayette Railroad tracks.

Arriving at Michigan City, Indiana, at 8:00 A.M., the train rolled to a stop under a magnificent, soaring funeral arch. An impromptu funeral service was held there, then the train was reconfigured and sent down the Michigan Central Railroad tracks. Engineer Edward Wilcox would pilot the Ranger to Chicago.

The train arrived in Chicago at 11:00 A.M., Monday, May 1. The city had a special bond with the Lincolns, and Chicagoans were going to give the late president one of the grandest farewells yet. The train slowed to a stop beside a specially erected platform just north of Twelfth Street. The casket was removed and placed on a bier in the center of a magnificent—if not pretentious—Gothic funeral arch erected on Michigan Avenue. Locomotive no. 58, piloted by James Colting of the Chicago & Alton Railroad, backed the train onto a trestle extending into Lake Michigan. This was at the city's primary lakefront railroad facilities. Once parked on the trestle, no. 58 began clanging its bell slowly, mournfully. It seems most men in charge of ringing a locomotive's bell either during arrival or departure did so on the count of eight. Count to eight—ring! Count to eight—ring!

The bell atop the Cook County Courthouse had been clanging incessantly, alerting citizens of the train's arrival. No one spoke as the casket was placed on the bier in the large center arch. The Western Light Band performed the "Lincoln Requiem," written specifically for the occasion. Thirty-six high school girls dressed in white with black sashes—again, representing the number of states—walked around the casket, each placing a garland near it.

Pallbearers then lifted the casket to the hearse, and the funeral cortege started down Michigan Avenue. There were probably one hundred fifty thousand Chicagoans lining the streets as the procession moved toward the courthouse. A forest of colorful flags, banners, and pennants moved slowly down the avenue amid the playing of dirges. Raised sabers and swords sparkled in the noon light. Husbands and wives wept against each other's shoulders. Many children, impressed by the spectacle, nonetheless turned sad thoughts to little Willie, in his casket on the train. They were glad he was being protected by loyal honor guards.

The line of mourners ascending the courthouse steps was immense. Viewing continued for twenty-eight hours, ending at 8:00 P.M., May 2. Another huge procession, illuminated by hundreds of torches, bore the remains back to the station. This time the procession moved west on Madison Street to Market Street and eventually turned south on Canal Street, arriving at the Chicago & Alton depot. As the train was prepared for the final leg of its journey to Springfield, the area around the depot was filled with the singing of a three-hundred-voice German choir.

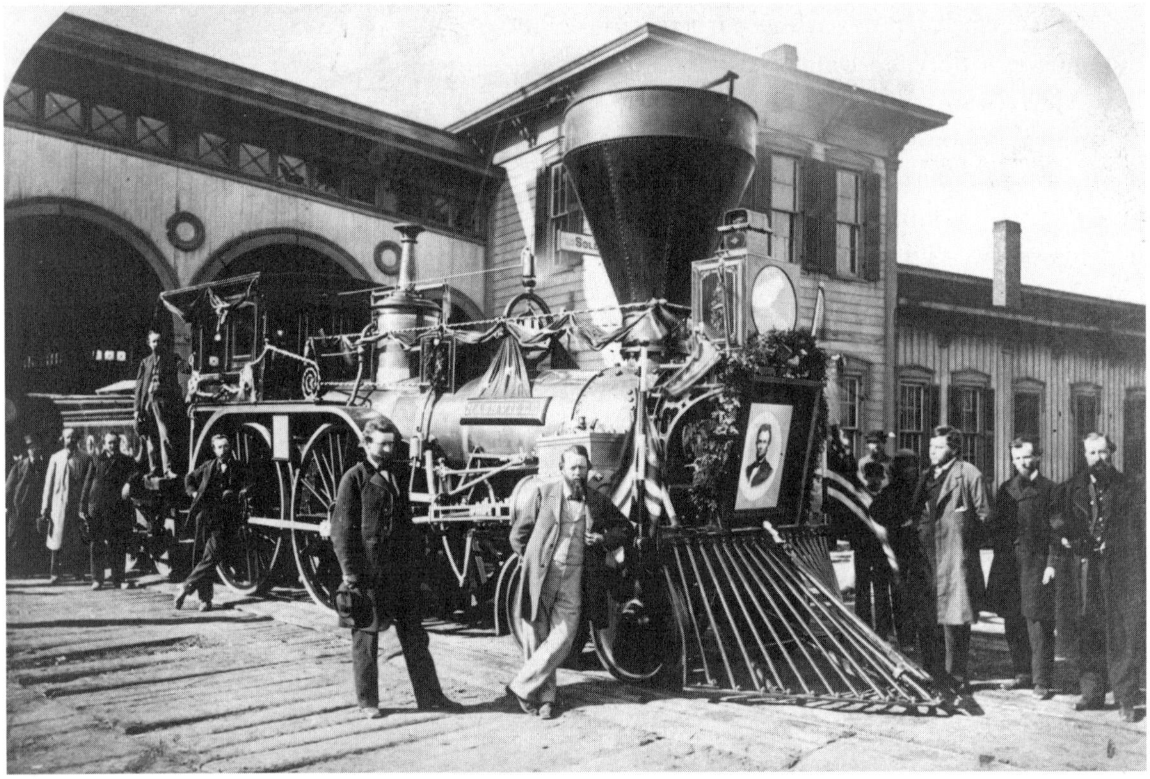

One of the most noted photos of the funeral train shows the crew and officials around the richly decorated Nashville at the Cleveland railroad facilities during that city's funeral.
(*Library of Congress*)

The locomotive L. Chase pulled the train to Cleveland's Union Station, arriving at 6:50 A.M. on Friday, April 28. The Dispatch pulled it from there to the Euclid Avenue Station. Union Station, seen in this 1866 image, was nearing completion when the train arrived.
(*Author's collection*)

Polished and its decorations fluffed up, the Nashville poses proudly at Cleveland's Union Station awaiting the next leg of the journey. (*Library of Congress*)

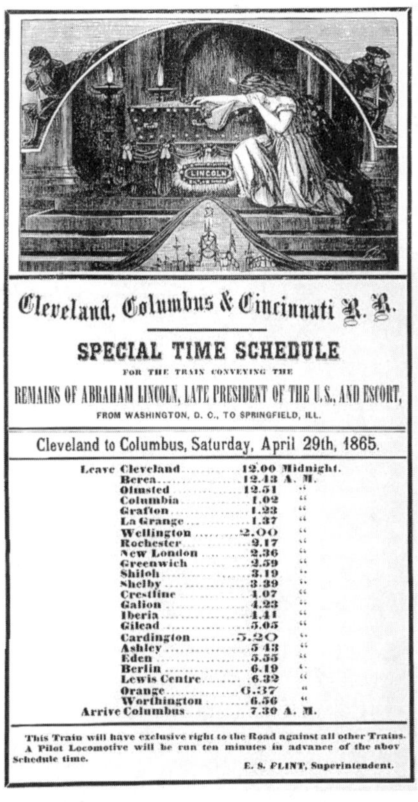

Cleveland, Columbus & Cincinnati R. R.

SPECIAL TIME SCHEDULE

FOR THE TRAIN CONVEYING THE

REMAINS OF ABRAHAM LINCOLN, LATE PRESIDENT OF THE U.S., AND ESCORT,

FROM WASHINGTON, D. C., TO SPRINGFIELD, ILL.

Cleveland to Columbus, Saturday, April 29th, 1865.

Leave	Cleveland	12.00	Midnight.
	Berea	12.43	A. M.
	Olmsted	12.51	"
	Columbia	1.02	"
	Grafton	1.23	"
	La Grange	1.37	"
	Wellington	2.00	"
	Rochester	2.17	"
	New London	2.36	"
	Greenwich	2.59	"
	Shiloh	3.19	"
	Shelby	3.39	"
	Crestline	4.07	"
	Galion	4.23	"
	Iberia	4.41	"
	Gilead	5.05	"
	Cardington	5.20	"
	Ashley	5 43	"
	Eden	5.55	"
	Berlin	6.19	"
	Lewis Centre	6.32	"
	Orange	6.37	"
	Worthington	6.56	"
Arrive	Columbus	7.30	A. M.

This Train will have exclusive right to the Road against all other Trains.
A Pilot Locomotive will be run ten minutes in advance of the abov Schedule time.

E. S. FLINT, Superintendent.

The schedule of the Cleveland, Columbus & Cincinnati Railroad shows the twenty-two stops to be made between the midnight departure from Cleveland to the 7:00 A.M. arrival at Columbus, Ohio. Some stops were as brief as eleven minutes. The Louisville handled the pilot train, with the Nashville following ten minutes behind.
(*Author's collection*)

The railyard beside Cleveland's Union Station—or depot, as it was often referred to—is quiet in this late-day image taken during the funeral stop. The loco on the left is credited with rearranging the Lincoln Special cars, dropping off some and bringing on others. (*Courtesy Christopher Busta-Peck*)

Upon the 7:20 A.M. arrival at Cleveland's Euclid Avenue Station, pallbearers placed the casket in the waiting hearse. A thirty-six-gun salute got the cortege moving. In this image, the hearse is moving up Euclid Avenue. (*Courtesy Christopher Busta-Peck*)

Because no building was large enough to handle the huge crowds expected for viewing the president's body, the Cleveland funeral committee had a large, pagoda-styled pavilion built in Monument Square. At top, the hearse has arrived with the casket. Below, another view of the solemn event in Cleveland's Monument Square. (*Author's collection*)

Throngs have gathered along the perimeter of the square. Many have opened umbrellas, as a soft rain is falling. The president's casket is being prepared inside the pavilion for public viewing. The embalmer was along to keep the corpse presentable, as discoloration was setting in. The pavilion is elaborately festooned with large plumes, flags, and black and white fabric twisted around the supports. (*Author's collection*)

A bird's-eye view of the pavilion in Monument Square (later Public Square). (*Author's collection*)

Most of the primary locomotives used during the run of the Lincoln Special have been historically noted, but others were involved in operations, particularly in the cities where cars were added or removed. Locos were used to move the train between railroads. The Chicago (pictured here) of the Cleveland, Columbus & Cincinnati Railroad is credited with maneuvers at the Cleveland railhead. (*Author's collection*)

The Louisville of the Cleveland, Columbus & Cincinnati Railroad headed the pilot train from Cleveland to Columbus. This is one of the few photos of the locomotives that pulled the pilot train during the funeral. Special trains were hastily assembled to transport dignitaries to the bigger city funerals. (*Author's collection*)

The scene outside the statehouse in Iowa City, Iowa, on April 19, 1865, when a memorial service was held.
(*Author's collection*)

Union Station in Columbus, Ohio, was opened in 1851. This photo is dated 1864, but the clerestory-roofed coaches outside the train shed put it close to 1870. The funeral train left Cleveland at midnight. Pulled by the Nashville, it traveled southwest overnight, reaching Columbus's Union Station at 7:30 A.M., April 29. A military escort placed the casket on a large, specially built hearse. Six horses pulled it to the statehouse for public viewing of Lincoln's body.
(*Author's collection*)

Guards with sabers keep dutiful watch over the car in the yard at Columbus in this carte de visite. The car was guarded twenty-four hours a day. The president's remains were on display at the statehouse, but Willie's casket remained on the car, more reason for constant guarding. (*Author's collection*)

Heavy rains had just ceased and the skies began to brighten as the train pulled into Columbus. The seventeen-foot-long hearse with the casket is on High Street, headed for the Capitol. "Lincoln" was emblazoned in silver capital letters on both sides of the vehicle. Spring flowers were thrown along the procession route, and lilac blooms were tossed under the wheels of the hearse. (*Author's collection*)

Columbus was one of thirteen cities to organize a major funeral. Here the procession has halted, and the hearse is stopped in front of the walkway up to the statehouse. In the upper right, the casket is being brought to the building. (*Author's collection*)

The Greek Doric columns of the Capitol colonnade are bound with black fabric. Barely visible are two flags at half-staff above the pediment and a plaque in the center that reads, "With malice to no one, with charity for all." Brooding onlookers watch the huge crowd waiting on the walkway and steps for their turn to enter. (*Author's collection*)

Guards stand at attention at both ends of the casket in the rotunda of the Columbus statehouse. A simple bier to hold the casket was chosen over the elaborate pagodas and catafalques used elsewhere. The casket is covered with spring blossoms, including an abundance of lilacs, to mask the odors emanating from the corpse. Many who viewed the president during this funeral later came to associate the scent of lilacs with the event. Some found the scent of lilacs repellant because of the sad memories it evoked. (*Author's collection*)

A wonderful illustration of the Columbus obsequies captures the majesty and solemnity of the occasion. (*Author's collection*)

The Sehrimer Building in Columbus is decorated in mournful bunting. The building was on South High Street. The horse-drawn trolley provided service to Union Station. (*Author's collection*)

The National Bank in Columbus is decorated for the funeral. All businesses along the funeral route were ordered closed by mayors in towns and cities during obsequies. Those businesses that did not close as a form of protest against Lincoln's legacy drew the wrath of a highly emotional citizenry. They could expect broken windows and beatings of employees. (*Courtesy Christopher Busta-Peck*)

Flamboyant entertainer and chair maker Seth Kinman once played a fiddle made of a mule's skull for Lincoln. He accompanied the president's remains as far as Columbus, marching in all the processions in his noted buckskins and fur hat. He made chairs from bones and antlers for several presidents. Here he sits in the one he made for Andrew Johnson, proudly holding his famous rifle, "Ol' Cottonblossum." (*Library of Congress*)

At 3:10 A.M. on April 30, over ten thousand people gathered at the Air Line Railroad Station in Richmond, Indiana, pictured in this postwar image. An impressive flowered arch spanned the tracks, and the sturdy, barrel-roofed station was adorned with flags, linked wreaths, and draping banners of red, white, and blue fabric. All locomotives at the facility were brought up and parked. When the funeral train arrived, the locos were illuminated and their bells were set to clanging. (*Author's collection*)

Indianapolis received the funeral train at 7:00 A.M., April 30, fifteen days after the president died. The casket, visible in the hearse, was taken to the statehouse. Some people found the peculiar entrance, obviously inspired by the delicate pagodas used in other cities, to be ponderous, unnecessary, and unattractive. (*Author's collection*)

The Indiana Capitol is visible in this broader view. (*Author's collection*)

It had rained so hard in Indianapolis that the procession was canceled. Here is a view of the hearse with its horses and grooms. The first group to pass Lincoln lying in state that day included five thousand children from different Sunday schools. Among them were many African American children. (*Author's collection*)

A closer look at the hearse used during the Indianapolis funeral. (*Author's collection*)

Citizens of Ravenna, Ohio, are gathered outside the decorated courthouse and adjacent jail to discuss the impact of the assassination. The funeral train was in Ohio when this carte de visite image was produced. (*Courtesy Christopher Busta-Peck*)

The Phoenix Block in Ravenna, Ohio, is suitably decorated to reflect the sentiments of citizens. (*Courtesy Christopher Busta-Peck*)

While en route to Chicago, the train stopped at Michigan City, Indiana, on the morning of May 1, and an impromptu funeral was held. The car the United States is beneath the arch. (*Author's collection*)

The arch at Michigan City was thirty feet tall and twenty-five feet wide. It was fret with roses, wreaths, and evergreen boughs, much of it the handiwork of the ladies of the city. An inscription, "Though dead he yet speaketh," was printed in large letters on white cloth stretched across the arch. They could only hope that the slain Lincoln yet speaketh. The country had deep problems to deal with, and the loss of his leadership was deeply troubling. (*Author's collection*)

A postwar view of the Michigan City station (left). (*Author's collection*)

A crowd is gathered in Court House Square in Bloomington, Illinois, participating in an indignation meeting, one of many held across the country to express grief and outrage over the killing of the president. (*Author's collection*)

A Civil War-era view of Chicago's waterfront railroad facilities, which accepted the funeral train May 1. The Illinois Central Railroad's massive train shed is left of center. (*Author's collection*)

A closer view of the Illinois Central train shed from the Civil War era. (*Author's collection*)

The funeral train, headed by Chicago & Alton Railroad locomotive no. 58, arrived in Chicago at 11:00 A.M. With its bell clanging mournfully, the train was backed onto a trestle in Lake Michigan. Locomotive no. 58 would handle the last leg of the journey—Chicago to Springfield. (*Author's collection*)

Lincoln was back in his beloved Illinois, but he couldn't be put to rest just yet. Chicagoans gave him a sendoff grander than those in Washington and New York City. The somewhat pretentious memorial arch and the decorations for the courthouse alone cost $15,000. With the casket in the hearse, the procession is about to get under way down Michigan Avenue. (*Library of Congress*)

Details from the previous photograph. The funeral train is in the background, with Lake Michigan beyond it.

The casket in the magnificent hearse.

The procession arrives at the Cook County Courthouse on May 1. (*Author's collection*)

The bell atop the courthouse announced to Chicago that Lincoln's remains had arrived. A steady stream of mourners is seen leaving via the courthouse steps. As many as seven thousand people passed the casket each hour. (*Library of Congress*)

An illustration depicts the scene inside the courthouse. (*Author's collection*)

Dozens of workers used scaffolds and ladders to apply the fantastic decorations to the courthouse tower. Viewing was still under way when this photo was taken. (*Author's collection*)

UPON THE MOMENT OF THE ARRIVAL
OF THIS SACRED RELIC IN THE CITY

FOURTEEN
SALUTES FROM CANNON

WILL BOOM FORTH A WELCOME

One for each letter forming the name

ABRAHAM LINCOLN

and one following each hour throughout the entire day.

Bands will Play National and
Sacred Airs, and Bells will Toll

The Public are requested to join in this demonstration
in honor of the event and in memory of the

WORLD'S GREATEST CHARACTER

Hang Out Flags and Drape
Your Homes in Mourning.

BE AN AMERICAN

and instill into your children and your children's children
the principles of this great and good man.

"With Malice Toward None. With Charity For All"

CHICAGO AND ALTON R. R. THE ONLY WAY.

The Chicago & Alton Railroad issued this forceful broadside detailing the conduct expected from citizens. (*Author's collection*)

The United States stands guarded in Chicago. It is believed the car coupled to it is the Pioneer, built by the Pullman Company. The luxurious car was added for the last leg of the journey, to Springfield. It was a wise move for Pullman to provide the car because it drew a lot of attention. (*Author's collection*)

This view of the United States in Chicago is among the most famous of the funeral. (*Library of Congress*)

A close-up of the car reveals rich details, such as the mourning decorations neatly attached with tassels. The artist's rendering of America's coat of arms in the oval had come into question. Some felt the eagle looked more like a turkey. (*Library of Congress*)

Handsome and bedecked, locomotive no. 58 suns itself in Chicago, with the train coupled and ready to leave. (*Author's collection*)

FOUR

"HERO, MARTYR, FRIEND, FAREWELL"

While the Chicago procession was taking the casket to the Canal Street station, officials of the Chicago & Alton Railroad took extra precautions for the safety of the train. Guards and watchmen with red and white signals were sent to all the wooden bridges to guard against fires. There had been threats of terrorism against the train since it left Washington. The switch tracks at remote and obscure sidings were spiked firmly closed (probably to prevent mischief by boys as much as by terrorists). All trains traversing the railroad were ordered to enter the nearest siding one hour before the scheduled time of the funeral train and remain there until it passed.

William S. Porter was a young brakeman on the Chicago & Alton during the event. Here are some of his memories, as provided in the *Illinois State Historical Society Journal*:

> The two locomotives selected for this honor (pulling the pilot and funeral train) were No. 40 and No. 57 [actually 58]. Both engines were of the same type and size (16 by 22-in cylinders), built by the Walter McQueen locomotive works at Schenectady, New York. They were wood burners with an old fashioned balloon smoke-stack, Russia iron jackets, brass dome, brass sand box, brass bell frame, six inch brass bands encircling the boiler about four feet apart for its entire length, brass hand railings along the running boards on both sides of the engine, and all highly polished.

Porter also provided interesting details of the guard of honor:

> A crack New York City regiment of soldiers escorted the body and performed guard duty over the entire trip. The guards on duty were placed in this manner: Four guards were posted in each car, two at each end. The moment the train stopped the guards came out of the car and took the positions assigned to them at the foot of the car steps and on both sides of the train. No one was allowed to board the train without a permit. When the signal to proceed was given the engineer gave two short blasts on the whistle, then the guards would mount the steps and stand there until the train got under way, then go inside and sit down.

And Porter gave this vivid description of the return procession:

> The hearse was drawn by eight large, coal black stallions. Each horse was accompanied by a groom who walked alongside with his hand on the bridle bit. The grooms were all Negroes, large and fine looking, and all were uniformed alike. They made an impressive appearance.

While the return procession was under way, the engine crews worked at prepping and firing the locos. The firebox door was opened, and more wood, and possibly a few pieces of coal, were tossed onto a small, simmering fire. Pulling notched levers that came up through the cab floor opened the dampers. A turn of a valve on the forced draft pipe leading into the smokestack would get the fire roaring. The sand domes were filled, and a trip by the water stations topped off the tenders.

It was then time to keep a watchful eye on the steam gauge. It took 125 pounds per square inch (psi) of steam pressure to get the locomotive moving. A glass tube water gauge on the backhead showed the water level. Alongside the engines, crewmen unscrewed grease caps and filled the steam chest with oil. Long-neck oilcans were used to reach inside the valve and drive linkage. Virtually anything that moved got a fresh squirt of oil.

Again, William Porter recalled the activity at the Canal Street Station: "On the evening of May 2, the two locomotives and train were backed into the Union Station, ready to take the road on their way to Springfield, Illinois, its final destination."

It was at Chicago that the first Pullman sleeping car, the Pioneer, was added to the train. It was built in Chicago at a cost of nearly twenty thousand dollars. Chicago was the rail capital of the North. George Pullman, an ambitious entrepreneur in his early thirties, hoped to capitalize on a growing wealthier class in a prosperous rail-dominated economy. Including it in the Lincoln Special was brilliant. The car received international attention.

By day the Pioneer was a posh parlor car. At night it resembled an upper-class hotel room. Being longer, taller, and wider than most cars, it was initially shunned by railroads because it required resizing of bridges and station platforms. The Pioneer could sleep up to fifty-seven passengers. The interior featured a carpeted floor and walls; plush upholstery; silver-, brass-, and nickel-plated adornments; exotic woods; heaters; fancy oil lamps; and an enameled ceiling. Like the United States, it rode on four trucks. Yardmen didn't like it because it, too, had trouble moving through switches. Numerous accounts of the funeral train state the Chicago & Alton quickly modified its bridges and station platforms to accommodate the car during the funeral. The railroad had actually made those improvements during an upgrade of the entire railroad well before the assassination.

When the pilot train was ten minutes down the line, the yardman checked his pocket watch and waved his signal lantern, giving the all clear. Somewhere, probably from the conductor, a bone pocket whistle was sounded. Engineer Henry Russell checked that the heavy reverse lever was released and then sat in his chair. The throttle was in front of him. It was a large lever that extended down through a heavy arched sector with notches. With the engine steamed up and the gauge reading 125 psi, Russell grasped the throttle lever at its top. A spring-loaded clasp pulled the ratchet out, and he pushed the throttle forward. The bell cord ran through a hole in the cab's front wall and then through pulleys above the fireman's seat. The fireman immediately tugged it, probably counting to eight between each pull. Russell then gave the whistle cord running over his head two quick pulls.

At 9:30 P.M., the Lincoln Special rolled smoothly out of Union Station. It gradually left the illumination of the city though the Bridgeport district along Chicago's South Side. As always, people watched silently, holding torches or standing beside bonfires as the train passed. The stations at Summit, Willow Springs, and Lamont were crowded with mourners.

William Porter, carefully tending his brake wheel, observed:

> At all the larger places like Joliet, Wilmington, Bloomington and Lincoln, there were large crowds of people congregated—stern, grim visaged men, tear bedimmed women and children—all silent, but with an anxious, expectant look, as of some impending disaster. It was that way all along the line. There were throngs of people at all the smaller towns, also, at the country road crossings could be seen a group of people waiting to see the arrival and passage of this train, the remembrance of which was to become the epoch of their lives.

At Lockport, a sign read, "Come Home." A crowd of at least twelve thousand stood in the rain, awaiting the midnight arrival at Joliet.

The Lincoln Special arrived in Springfield at 9:00 A.M., May 3. Reportedly, it maneuvered briefly near the Great Western Railroad depot. The famous depot, often used by the Lincolns, was only two blocks from their home. Abe had launched his inaugural train ride there.

The train stopped at the Chicago & Alton depot, where a crowd extended two miles north along the tracks. In his book *Lincoln Memorial: The Journeys of Abraham Lincoln*, William T. Coggeshall quoted a reporter for the *New York Tribune* as writing:

> The train that brought him to his long home moved slowly into town, moved slowly through the masses of plain people who had come from all the country round about. The train stops. The pallbearers, those old men, friends of his, lang syne, approach. The stillness among all the people is painful, but when the coffin is taken from the car, that stillness is broken by sobs and these are more painful than the stillness.

Nearly every building in Springfield's commercial district was decorated. All the churches anticipated full attendance when services started. And of course pretty much everyone was wearing black. Mourning ribbons were worn on most arms.

The tradition of wearing black and draping structures in black during mourning periods is said to have started in Tonga, a Polynesian state. Wearing black clothing was a tradition in the Roman Empire as well. On the matter of public grieving, America, in spite of its then sense of newness, looked to the Georgian and Victorian eras and their complex traditions regarding mourning. In medieval Europe, it was common for widowed queens to wear white as a show of intense mourning. In 1393, Parisians witnessed a royal funeral in which all the participants wore white.

Mary Lincoln received a heartfelt letter from Britain's Queen Victoria after the assassination. The queen had undergone a long, striking, and public grieving period four years earlier following the death of her husband, Prince Albert. Each woman was devastated by her loss. Mary did not want to be as conspicuous in her grief as the queen, however, and became nearly reclusive. She and the queen had something else in common: their husbands shared a revulsion of slavery. Prince Albert was at one time early in their marriage president of the Society for the Extinction of Slavery.

Of the events in Springfield, Walter Barlow Stevens related in his book, *A Reporter's Lincoln*, what witness Robert Wilson McClaughrey experienced:

> The most pathetic sight to me was the intense grief manifested by the colored people, thousands of whom had journeyed for days in order to be in Springfield at the funeral. In addition to their section in the procession, they were assigned a place extending from the then city limits toward the cemetery and there thousands of them massed. Every one of them, it seemed, had possessed himself or herself of some badge or token, which would indicate their grief. Sometimes it was a simple piece of black cloth or crepe, not larger than a man's hand. All who could afford it had clothed themselves in black and as the bier passed, almost every one of them either knelt or prostrated himself or herself upon the ground and gave way to touching demonstrations of grief. They well knew that their greatest friend was passing to his rest, and the future seemed dark enough to their vision.

The sadness in Springfield was not hyped by the lavish national spectacle preceding it. Here it was deep and profound. Lincoln was their favorite son. They loved him. He had always been kind, neighborly, and decent to them—not to mention how skillfully he handled their legal problems.

Lincoln's law partner, William H. Herndon, described the scene that day:

> The funeral train reached Springfield on the 3rd of May. The casket was borne to the State House and placed in Representative Hall—the very chamber in which in 1854, the deceased had pronounced that fearful invective against the sin of human slavery. The doors were thrown open, the coffin lid was removed, and we who had known the illustrious dead in other days, and before the nation lay its claim upon him, moved sadly through and looked for the last time on the silent, upturned face of our departed friend. All day long and through the night a stream of people filed reverently to the catafalque. Some of them were his colleagues at the bar, some his old friends from New Salem; some crippled soldiers from the battlefields of the war and some were little children who, scarce realizing the impressiveness of the scene, were destined to live and tell their children yet to be born the sad story of Lincoln's death.

Indeed, the sadness in Springfield was singular, as Herndon pointed out. There was a family atmosphere to the thing. Springfielders felt detached from the rest of the country. The North had won the war, but there was a powerful sense of defeat in the faces watching the procession. That attitude persisted since the assassination even though the antebellum South lay in ruins, its traditional way of life finished, its romanticism vaporized, its cherished sons moldering in common graves.

In Springfield, the longing for Lincoln was terrible and heartrending. It was shattering, imagining the murder and Mary pulling him close to her. The hope for resurrection of the man was halted by the stark, silent emptiness and finality of death. No—not the most soulful praying, the most ardent tears, could bring Old Abe back. They never come back—the dead.

The Capitol had been gloriously decorated for the event. Victor Wheeler was sixteen when news of the assassination reached Springfield. He was a member of the 146th Illinois Infantry at the time and was given the duty of helping prepare the statehouse for the funeral. He would also follow the casket to the cemetery, tramping with his regiment, and then stand at attention during the service outside the vault. He saw the two remaining Lincoln sons near the vault, the subjects of much affection from those around them.

Wheeler became part of a group of thirty men chosen to decorate the statehouse. He and Isaac "Ike" Andrews, a young man from Freeport, were charged with decorating the dome, they being agile and therefore the only two capable of working at such heights. They did a remarkable job, attaching the long streamers and rosettes. Andrews and another young man were then sent over to drape the Lincolns' former home. Their zeal was evident. They did a splendid job and received hearty compliments for their work.

At times, as many as 150 people were involved in decorating the statehouse. Women were deeply involved. The building was much loved, being, as it were, the social center of the city.

Lincoln was twenty-eight back in 1837, when construction on the Capitol started. He watched the first large blocks of yellow limestone being hauled to the site from a quarry seven miles outside of town. The strapping rail-splitter was a model of self-improvement. He was self-educated and naturally brilliant, and books were his Internet. He knew books could change the world: the Bible, *The Communist Manifesto* in 1848, *Uncle Tom's Cabin*, published in 1852.

About fifteen hundred yards of black and white goods went into decorating the statehouse. It was in that building in June 1858 that Lincoln gave his famous "House Divided" speech. One thousand Republican delegates were present, and they had just chosen Lincoln as their candidate for US Senate to run against Stephen A. Douglas.

The speech awakened the nation to the coming perils of continued slavery. The regional hemorrhaging had already begun, starting in 1854 with the violent border confrontations over slavery in the Kansas Territory. In his famous speech, Lincoln warned, "A house divided against itself cannot stand. . . . Either the opponents of slavery will arrest the further spread of it, and place it where the public mind shall rest in the belief that it is in the course of ultimate extinction: or its advocates will push it forward, till it shall become alike lawful in all the states, old as well as new—North as well as South."

Lincoln now lay in state in the building where he made that speech only nine years earlier. A lot had happened since then. His law partner, Herndon, said the speech cost him the Senate election but made him president. In the two days Lincoln's casket lay within the catafalque, seventy-five thousand filed past, paying their final tribute.

On Thursday, May 4, at 10:00 A.M., the casket was closed and carried out of the building. As it was placed in the hearse, a choir of 250 voices sang hymns, "Peace, Troubled Soul" among them. The funeral cortege began its slow march to Oak Ridge Cemetery. What followed was an allegory of grief, a study in black dress and bunting, of Lincoln's horse, Old Bob, being led riderless in the procession, of drawn sabers and groupings of flags moving like masts ahead of delegates and soldiers. Everything turned west onto Third Street and continued down the dirt road to the eastern gate of the cemetery. The procession passed under a floral arch and proceeded to the receiving vault. Willie's casket had already been placed inside. His brothers, Robert and Tad, waited outside, tended by loving family and friends. Their mother did not attend. As the casket was consigned to the vault, the choir sang additional hymns, among them "Unveil Thy Bosom, Faithful Tomb" and "Take This New Treasure to Thy Trust."

Chicago-based Bishop Mathew Simpson of the Methodist Episcopal Church had always been admired by the Lincolns. In his stirring address, he concluded:

> Chieftain, farewell. The nation mourns thee. Mothers shall teach thy name to their lisping children. The youth of our land shall emulate thy virtues. Statesmen shall study thy record, and learn lessons of wisdom. Mute though thy lips be, yet they still speak. Hushed is thy voice, but its echoes of liberty are ringing through the world, and the sons of bondage listen with joy. Prisoned thou art in death, and yet thou art marching abroad, and chains and manacles are bursting at thy touch. Thou didst fall not for thyself. The assassin had no hate for thee. Our hearts were aimed at, our national life was sought. We crown thee as our martyr, and humanity enthrones thee as her triumphant son. Hero, martyr, friend, farewell.

When it was over—finally over—and all the flowers lay rotting in the streets and all the black bunting was tugged down, Mary, so inconspicuous during the twenty-day grand funeral, made her way to the vault, there to twist in bewildering heartache. The pain was vast. She probably ignored the great conceptualizing by some participants in the grand civic, musical, and religious pageant. At least seven million witnessed some part of it, but that didn't matter to her. All the hidden, perceived meanings in it, either of personal or national significance, meant nothing. The preachers pondering in their sermons why God permitted the assassination at all, let alone on Good Friday, had not the power to quell her suffering. In the silence of the wooded cemetery, where branches thickened with spring life, Mary ached for the man she loved. The blood and agony of the last four years aside, the freeing of a race from slavery aside, the temporary abatement of her own tormenting demons aside, Mary's emotions may, for a moment, have run sweetly pure, and, alone in the darkness of the vault, she wept.

The funeral train brought Lincoln and son Willie home to Springfield on May 3, 1865. It stopped at the Great Western depot. It was here that Lincoln had made a heartfelt farewell speech from the back platform of his first inaugural train. (*Author's collection*)

Mourners linger near Springfield's Chicago & Alton Railroad station on Jefferson Street. It is decorated for the funeral service. Both this and the Great Western depot were involved in the arrival of the train. The pilot train arrived at 8:50 A.M., with the funeral train rolling in at 9:00 A.M. The Lincoln Special had made its last stop. (*Author's collection*)

Adorned with plumes and bunting, Springfield's hearse was one of the finest used in the funeral. Hearses are among the most sophisticated vehicles built. Fine woods, etched glass, brass and silver attachments, and lush upholstery can make them stunning. (*Library of Congress*)

The Lincolns' Springfield home decorated for the funeral services. (*Author's collection*)

A photo of the Lincoln home taken at a happier time shows Abraham on the lawn with one son behind him and his other two sons on the sidewalk. (*Author's collection*)

During their time in Springfield, the Lincolns worshiped at First Presbyterian Church. (*Author's collection*)

Lincoln's Springfield horse was variously called Old Bob or Old Robin. The family home, in funeral regalia, is in the background. Old Bob was used in the funeral cortege, led as a riderless horse. (*Author's collection*)

When the Lincolns left Springfield for Washington, they gave their dog, Fido, to a neighbor. Fido was brought out for the procession. Abraham loved animals, especially kittens. Secretary of State William Seward gave the Lincolns two kittens early in his first term. (*Author's collection*)

The Globe Tavern in downtown Springfield served as a boardinghouse, tavern, and offices for several stage lines. A clerk rang a bell mounted on the roof to alert stablemen that a stage was arriving. They then ran out and tended the horses. The Globe was a favorite place for newlyweds to spend the first years of their marriage. That was the case with Abe and Mary Lincoln. They took up room and board for four dollars a week after their wedding in 1842. Their son Robert was born there. (*Author's collection*)

A view looking toward the Globe Tavern taken during the funeral services. Pallbearers and other prominent participants are gathered beside the tavern. (*Library of Congress*)

A close-up of the pallbearers reveals many Lincoln look-alikes. (*Library of Congress*)

A bird's-eye view of downtown Springfield during the Civil War. The arrow right of center points to the Lincoln-Herndon law office on Adams Street. Lincoln and partner Stephen T. Logan practiced law in a third-floor office. When that partnership dissolved in 1844, Lincoln took on a young lawyer, William H. Herndon, as a junior partner. They practiced law until 1852. (*Author's collection*)

Lincoln's law office decorated during the funeral. (*Author's collection*)

Nowhere was the sorrow felt more deeply than in Springfield. This is a view the day of the procession. (*Author's collection*)

For ten days, as many as 150 men and women swarmed over the Capitol, decorating it with up to fifteen hundred yards of black and white goods. (*Author's collection*)

A large, pagoda-style tent was erected over the dais in the rotunda. This is a rare interior view of the funeral. (*Author's collection*)

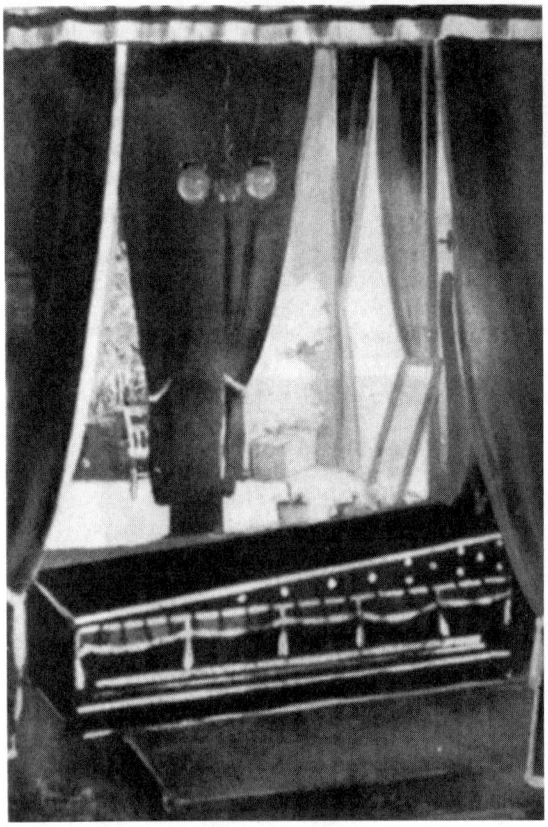

The bier inside the rotunda.
(*Author's collection*)

The Springfield City Council voted April 19 to allocate $20,000 for the funeral. This picture shows the elaborately decorated Capitol building with a crowd gathered out front.
(*Author's collection*)

Mourners wait in line to enter the Capitol through the north door for viewing. (*Author's collection*)

Another view of the crowds in Springfield.
(*Author's collection*)

After viewing Lincoln's remains, citizens left through the south door.
(*Author's collection*)

A funeral arch was erected at the entrance to Oak Ridge Cemetery, where Lincoln and Willie were entombed.
(*Author's collection*)

A crowd lingers in front of decorated commercial buildings on Springfield's Washington Street. The photo was taken on the east side of the public square.
(*Author's collection*)

Guards watch over the receiving vault where Lincoln and his son's remains were placed. The cemetery had a wild look. Some said Lincoln came from the wild and was returned to it. A more fitting tomb and memorial was planned. In 1871, the president's remains and those of his three youngest sons were placed in crypts in the unfinished tomb. The tomb was completed in 1874. (*Author's collection*)

A rare view of Abe and Willie's caskets inside the holding vault. (*Author's collection*)

The completed Lincoln Tomb is shown in relation to the holding vault at the base of a hill. Lincoln's and his three sons' remains were removed and returned to the tomb many times when the monument was going though repairs. (*Author's collection*)

Lincoln's remains were moved seventeen times, the result of numerous repairs to the tomb. Here his casket is set to the side during one of those repair periods. Eventually the cedar casket was placed in a steel-lined chamber dug beneath the sarcophagus room. The chamber was then filled with cement to discourage attempts to steal the corpse. (*Author's collection*)

The 117-foot-tall tomb now holds the remains of Abe, Mary, and their sons Edward, William, and Thomas. Their son Robert is buried in Arlington National Cemetery. (*Author's collection*)

FIVE

"I SAW TWO TALL AND STATELY PINES"

The assassination of President Lincoln had the potential to shatter an already fractured nation. People were terrified and paranoia swept the land. A president had never been killed before. John Ford permanently closed his Ford's Theatre, where the killing occurred. The $100,000 reward (equivalent to $1 million today) for information leading to the capture of the conspirators was unprecedented. The manhunt for John Wilkes Booth and his conspirators was likewise unprecedented, involving local sheriffs, marshals, and military units. Fortunately, they got them quickly. People who sympathized with the villains were beaten and some even killed. A prolonged search may have led to riots.

The spectacular national funeral continues to be analyzed, leading to perhaps too many overthought meanings. It is reasonable, though, to assume it had a healing effect. It managed to diminish thoughts of revenge by uniting Northerners in a collective grief. In glorious, nearly perfect, and spectacular fashion, Americans sent Old Abe off in grand style.

The world was impressed by the scope and spectacle of it as well. In a world ruled by kings and queens, perhaps it was too early to sound the death knell for this new, quirky, self-governing republic. Maybe the old monarchies perceived threats. America was horrified that its leader was murdered when European monarchies had been killing family members for advancement to the throne since medieval days. Shakespeare apprised us of their dastardliness with King Lear, Hamlet, and Macbeth. Americans proved they could pull together in a crisis. They approached this disaster with level-headedness and did not go off half-cocked.

Four years of savage war had sent a torrent of blood across the land. A river of tears washed that blood away. Broken hearts over dead sons did not lead to violent reprisal. The elegant, gentlemanly surrender between Grant and Lee at Appomattox was breathtaking. Southerners grudgingly accepted that they were a conquered people. They had cried a river of tears as well. Their infrastructure was in shambles. It was time to unite and rebuild. Although they found the lavish funeral vulgar, they realized the death of

Lincoln was a profound loss for them as well. Southerners expressed some of the sweetest, most heartfelt sentiments of grief.

Father Abe was a strange fellow, henpecked and burdened with the monumental task of keeping the country united. Yet he never lost his appealing commonness. The funeral elevated him to divine status, a sacred martyr—notions he probably would have laughed off. Nonetheless, he was a great man. Even his military enemies grieved. There is an unspoken respect—an eternal fellowship—among most warriors.

Lincoln's passing said a lot about national duty, self-sacrifice, courage, and putting others' needs ahead of our own. Lincoln was depressed and prematurely aged, and his service ultimately left his wife a war widow.

The funeral was a marvel of rapid mobilization, a fantastic accomplishment that should have made all Americans proud. And that dazzling train! Colorful, flag-bedecked, glitzy, and sublime, it rolled humbly through seven states and 180 cities and towns, projecting reassurance to a stricken people.

Black is mentioned unendingly in accounts: black clothes, black mourning cloth, black hearses and catafalques, black horses, plumes, crepe, and arm badges. But all that black was set within a universe of sparkling color—spring flowers; Old Glory waving from poles; silver stars and fringes; pretty girls wearing white dresses; white horses; green pine wreaths and garlands; and those beautiful locomotives with their brass fittings and red and green wheels. And there were the sounds: the firing of cannon, choirs singing, bells tolling, soldiers' boots tramping, and horses' hooves clattering on stone-paved streets.

As the funeral train headed back to Washington, it was gradually reduced as cars were returned to railroads that provided them. Slowly, it was defrocked of its bunting. When, finally, the United States arrived at Alexandria, Virginia, some of its funeral crepe was unraveled, packaged in a box, and sent to the Treasury Department, where it resides today in the department's archives.

If only the car itself could have been as lovingly tended to. Considered one of America's most sacred relics, it was subjected to humiliating stewardship. Forgotten, ignored, and left to vandals on a railroad siding, it perished in a prairie fire near Minneapolis in 1911.

The manhunt for Jefferson Davis ended shortly after the funeral. He was captured in Irwinville, Georgia, May 10. On May 19, 1865, he was imprisoned at Fortress Monroe in Virginia. He was roughly treated. Irons were riveted around his ankles, and he was denied visitors and books, except for the Bible.

President Andrew Johnson wanted nothing to do with putting Davis on trial for treason. That would hamper reconciliation efforts. There were no trials for treason at all in the end. Americans were fed up with the war. They wanted to move on.

Northern industrialist Cornelius "Commodore" Vanderbilt was among those who posted the $100,000 bail that got Davis freed in 1867. President Johnson issued full amnesty for the former Confederate leader in 1868.

Davis and his family wandered for a spell. He joined his beloved Varina and children in Montreal, Canada, where they had fled during the collapse of the Confederacy. They lived in Lennoxville, Quebec, until 1868, and then went to Cuba and later to Europe, where he looked for employment. The family moved back to America, to Memphis, Tennessee, in 1869, when Davis became president of the Carolina Life Insurance Company. Barred from federal office, he was nonetheless elected to the US Senate again but refused to serve.

Cautious in his opinions, he remained a racist through Reconstruction to the end of his life, believing blacks were inferior to whites. He opposed "Yankee and Negroe" rule over the South, as pointed out in William Cooper's biography of the Confederate president, *Jefferson Davis: American*, and threw in with other Southern supremacists who advocated white dominance of blacks.

He won renewed respect among ex-Confederates with his attendance at Lost Cause ceremonies, where large crowds cheered him. Such events spoke to some Southerners' inability to come to grips with reality. Far too many longed for the old days of slave and master. It was a terrible unreality that led to the rise of the Ku Klux Klan and racist policies in the postwar South.

Oddly hopeful about America's future, Davis nonetheless believed secession was constitutional. He took his love of the Confederacy to his death, which came December 6, 1889. He had Varina's hand in his when he died, just as Lincoln had his hand in Mary's the moment he was fatally shot.

Davis had survived his Northern counterpart by almost a quarter of a century. Not to be outdone, those loyal to Davis provided him with a lavish New Orleans funeral. In 1893, Varina Davis had his remains reinterred at Hollywood Cemetery in Richmond, Virginia. An impressive funeral train carried the remains to the former Confederate capital via the Louisville & Nashville Railroad.

Apparently, Lincoln's funeral had become the benchmark for grand farewells. Davis's was certainly impressive, being the largest ever held in the South to that time.

There was a tremendous national outpouring of grief over the death of former president Ulysses Grant in August 1885. The man who accepted Lee's surrender twenty years earlier had become the nation's most-loved veteran. His funeral rivaled Lincoln's.

On May 10, 1865, President Johnson declared an end to the war—though there were still a few hot spots to deal with—and ordered a Grand Review of the Armies. Held May 23–24 in the capital, it was an impressive affair and did much to calm the public a month after the assassination.

With the official end of the war, the railroads were again called on to handle demobilization. Tens of thousands of soldiers had to be returned to their homes. Many of them were wounded and had no money. Churches and women's societies sent members to the stations to await the trains. Upon arrival, they boarded the cars and cared for the wounded, giving them water and food and changing their bandages. They swatted away insects that tormented their oozing wounds. They spoke words of encouragement and gave money to those in need. Those too weak to cross town to make other rail connections were given free buggy rides.

A market for postmortem art and memorabilia arose after the war. This included stereoviews, cartes de visite, paintings, books, and something called skeletal bouquets—an eerily beautiful arrangement of chemically altered leaves. Lincoln was depicted heroically in many illustrations. Mary authorized a strange and controversial photo of her husband's spirit superimposed behind her. Some of the more touching creations were photos of women mourning, and most homes had at least one portrait of Lincoln on display.

After her husband's funeral, Mary Lincoln moved to Chicago with her two sons. In 1870, Congress granted the widow a pension of $3,000 a year for life—about $55,000 today. The press had resumed its tradition of being hard on her, which it had taken a brief respite from during the funeral. It had always been brutal to her and her husband. When Willie died, the press criticized Mary in a particularly cruel manner, saying at least she was there for her sons' deaths when other mothers were not there when their sons died on the battlefield.

Then tragedy struck again. In July 1871, son Tad died at age eighteen. The loss of her husband and three sons pitched Mary into deep grief and depression. Her behavior grew increasingly erratic and troubling.

Her last surviving son, Robert, was an up-and-coming Chicago lawyer. The burden of her care fell to him, and he became progressively alarmed at her disconcerting conduct. She was paranoid, belligerent, and highly demanding. She insisted on wearing only black years after her husband's death and walked around Chicago, for a time, with $56,000 in government bonds sewn into her petticoats even though she had no reason to fear poverty.

Her irrational behavior intensified, putting an undue burden on her son. Robert's wife, the former Mary Eunice Harlan, couldn't stand her and avoided her at all costs. She did not even attend her funeral. Fearing that his mother would harm herself, he arranged for an insanity trial in which he stated, "I have no doubt my mother is insane. She has long been a great source of anxiety for me." Seventeen witnesses testified to her unstable condition, and the court ruled in Robert's favor. Mary was committed to Bellevue Place, an upscale sanitarium, on May 20, 1875. While there, she publicly embarrassed Robert through a series of letters to the editor of the *Chicago Times*. The contents of the letters convinced the director of Bellevue that she was competent. The following, from Abraham Lincoln Online's "Mary Lincoln at Bellevue Place," explains what happened next:

> With the help of lawyers James and Myra Bradwell, Mary managed to engineer a release from her indefinite confinement in record speed. Myra told a Chicago newspaper reporter, "Mary Lincoln is no more insane than I am." Mary left Bellevue Place on September 11, 1875, when she was released into the custody of Ninian and Elizabeth Edwards. On June 15, 1876, Mary was officially declared sane in a Chicago court.

In 1876, she left for Europe, spending four years traveling and then residing in Pau, France. Deeply estranged from her son, she spent her final years in quiet agony. She took over-the-counter drugs commonly issued to women of her day. They contained alcohol and opium. Plagued with reduced eyesight from severe cataracts, she became prone to falling. A severe tumble off a stepladder in 1879 caused spinal injuries.

She remained estranged from Robert, although they may have reconciled briefly toward the end. On July 16, 1882, she had a stroke at her sister's residence, went into a coma, and died that morning. She was sixty-three.

Her half-sister, Emilie Todd-Helm, reminisced in Katherine Helm's 1928 book, *The True Story of Mary, Wife of Lincoln*:

> Any one could see that Mr. Lincoln admired Mary and was very proud of her. She took infinite pains to fascinate him again and again with pretty coquettish clothes and dainty little airs and graces. She was gay and light-hearted, hopeful and happy. She had a high temper and perhaps did not always have it under complete control, but what did it matter? Her little temper was soon over, and her husband loved her none the less, perhaps all the more, for this human frailty needed his love and patience to pet and coax the sunny smile to replace the sarcasm and tears—and oh, how she did love this man.

Mary Lincoln remains one of America's most distinctive figures, and one of its most tragic. She was difficult and eccentric but altogether harmless. It might be said that John Wilkes Booth killed her as well that night at Ford's Theatre. She never recovered emotionally. Twice she attempted suicide. In *Abraham Lincoln: From Skeptic to Prophet*, author Wayne C. Temple relates how Reverend Doctor James Armstrong Reed spoke of the Lincolns' inseparableness in his eulogy given at Springfield's Presbyterian Church, comparing them to two pines he saw in the Allegheny Mountains:

> I saw two tall and stately pines standing on a rocky ledge, where they had grown so closely together as to be virtually united at the base, their interlocking roots entering the same rock cavities, and penetrating the same soil. . . .
>
> But the taller of the two had, years before, been struck by a flash of lightning that had gone to its very roots, shattering it from top to bottom, and leaving it scarred and dead. . . .
>
> The other, apparently uninjured, had survived for some years, but it was evident from the appearance that it too was now quite dead. It had lingered in fellowship with its dead companion, but the shock was too much for it. In their sympathetic fellowship and union, both trees had suffered the same calamity. They had virtually been killed at the same time. With the one that lingered, it was only slow death from the same cause. So it seems today, that we are only at death placing his seal upon the lingering victim of a past calamity.

The country mourned her passing. Newspapers that had savaged her put illustrations of black mourning bands around their articles. Stores were closed in Springfield, and thousands of mourners, wearing black, lined the streets. She would have been pleased with all the fuss. It was a good send-off. Three days later, on July 19, 1882, her casket was put in the holding vault with her three sons and beloved husband.

Robert Lincoln intimated he never experienced the closeness with his father that his younger brothers enjoyed. He remembered that his father was away much of his youth, off on the judicial circuit. A singular memory of his father packing his saddlebags before riding off stayed with him much of his life. Robert was supposed to be with his parents at Ford's Theatre the night of the assassination but turned it down because of fatigue. He'd been at the battlefront much of the day. He personally wrote to President Andrew Johnson on April 25, 1865, asking the stressed commander in chief that his family be allowed to stay in the White House another two weeks. His mother simply could not leave yet. Johnson graciously accommodated them.

Following in his father's footsteps, Robert became a lawyer and then entered politics. He was courted to run for president several times but refused. In 1868, he married Mary Harlan. They had three children: Mary "Mamie" (1869–1939), Abraham Lincoln II (1873–1890), and Jessie Harlan Lincoln (1875–1948).

There were remarkable historical coincidences in Robert's life. As noted earlier, Edwin Booth, brother of his father's assassin, had saved him from serious injury or possible death. Also, Robert Lincoln was present at the shooting of two other presidents: James A. Garfield, on July 2, 1881, at the Sixth Street Train Station in Washington, DC, and William McKinley, on September 6, 1901, at the Pan-American Exposition in Buffalo, New York. Robert served as secretary of war from 1881 to 1885 under Presidents Garfield and Chester A. Arthur.

He had his father's love of railroads and was general counsel of the Pullman Palace Car Company. Following George Pullman's death in 1897, Robert became the company's president.

Robert built Hildene, a beautiful, Gilded Age mansion, for his family in Manchester, Vermont. This was one of several grand achievements for this tragic family. Its famous patriarch, Abraham, had emerged from a rustic cabin and ascended to the White House.

On July 26, 1926, Robert Todd Lincoln died in his sleep at age eighty-two at Hildene. He was buried in Arlington National Cemetery, the only member of his family not to be buried in the Springfield memorial tomb. His granddaughter, Mary Lincoln Beckwith, was the last Lincoln to occupy Hildene. She died there in 1975. The last person of direct Lincoln lineage died in 1985. That was Abraham and Mary's grandson Robert Todd Lincoln Beckwith.

Abraham Lincoln's casket was moved seventeen times before finally being sealed in a steel-lined chamber in the memorial tomb at Oak Ridge Cemetery. Repairs to the structure necessitated the many removals of the casket.

During a final massive reconstruction of the tomb in 1901, Lincoln's casket was opened to confirm he was still in there. After robbers tried to remove Lincoln's remains in 1876, rumors persisted for years that the body in the casket was not Lincoln's. It was decided to satisfy everyone's curiosity about this by opening part of the casket. On September 26, 1901, two plumbers cut through the lead lining of the casket and removed a section just above Lincoln's head and shoulders. Present was Joseph Lindley, a member of the guard of honor. Earlier he had summoned his fourteen-year-old son,

Fleetwood Lindley, from school so he could have a look as well.

The lid was removed and a harsh, choking odor arose from the casket. Twenty-three people, including Fleetwood, slowly approached and leaned over to view the remains. Lincoln was perfectly recognizable. His chest was covered with a yellow moss and remnants of a flag that had been placed on it. His gloves had rotted away. His face was a bronze color. His hair, beard, and mole were preserved, but his eyebrows were gone. The repeated embalming during the funeral may have left him partially mummified.

Fleetwood remembered this experience the rest of his life. He died February 1, 1963, being the last living person to have seen Lincoln's face. As an added honor, he was allowed to hold one of the straps used to lower the resealed casket into its final resting place, ten feet below the tomb floor. The chamber was then filled with four thousand pounds of portland cement.

Lincoln's earthly remains were now fixed. Locked deep in a block of stone, he was free from the sight and touch of those who would jostle him anymore. The awkwardness of being moved so many times would probably have inspired one of his funny stories. "Let me tell you how they moved Old Abe's casket seventeen times!" he might exclaim to his cabinet members. And they'd roll their eyes, lamenting they had to endure another of his tales.

He could rest in peace now, the folly of humanity parading above him and far past him into the future. In the hearts of those who still admire him—including many around the world—the hope that he may exist in some eternal realm is soothing. Maybe he is with Mary and they are gleefully watching their sons play in the yard with Fido. Their backs are to us, as they have long since wearied of humanity. Their indifference hurts because some lingering fascination—or maybe even affection—leaves us incapable of forgetting them.

In a deeply moving representation of the devastation felt on a personal level, Columbia grieves beside the slain president's casket. The heroic, goddesslike Columbia—whose name is derived from Christopher Columbus's—represents the female personification of the United States. (*Author's collection*)

A souvenir carte de visite titled "The Apotheosis of Lincoln." The martyred president is welcomed to heaven by George Washington, holding a laurel wreath over his head. In theology, apotheosis is the glorification or elevation of a human to divine status. (*Author's collection*)

Lady Liberty crowns her martyr in this highly romanticized souvenir. (*Author's collection*)

A carte de visite of a boy in military dress with a mourning ribbon on his jacket. (*Author's collection*)

This image of a heartbroken woman crying in a chair similar to the one Lincoln was shot in projects intense emotion and again speaks to the grief felt on a personal level. (*Author's collection*)

A play on the religious superstitions of the era, when séances and spiritualist mediums were used in attempts to contact the dead. Mary approved this gimmicky image of her husband's ghostly hands on her shoulders. In spite of the criticism she received, it evoked a deep emotional response in many people. (*Author's collection*)

An example of postmortem memorial art was skeleton leaves, or phantom bouquets. Leaves were submerged in chemicals that dissolved their pulpy matter until only the fibrous structure or skeleton remained. These were then bleached to a brilliant white in chloride of lime. The lacy creations were amazingly pure and beautiful. The process dates back to the Ming Dynasty in China. (*Author's collection*)

A twentieth-century postcard used an image taken April 16, 1865, the day after Lincoln died. It shows citizens in Vicksburg, Mississippi, honoring the fallen president. What was really in their minds didn't matter. With Southern cities occupied by federal troops, they were forced to pay respects with the tolling of bells, church sermons exalting Lincoln, and other shows of respect. In truth, Southerners were disgusted by the funeral, thinking it a slap in their faces, as if they were responsible as a whole for the murder. They also found the endless displaying of the corpse morbid and in bad taste. (*Author's collection*)

Although the train did not stop in Detroit, the city, like many others, held a mock funeral, complete with procession and memorial services. In this retouched photo, an enormous crowd has gathered in Martius Square on April 25, 1865, for a ceremony. (*Author's collection*)

Detroit's Phoenix steam fire engine no. 3 and its crew in front of the firehouse. The engine, decorated with strands of crepe, was featured in the mock funeral. (*Author's collection*)

Butler Street School in Bryan, Ohio, bears American flags in a modest but heartfelt tribute to Lincoln. (*Author's collection*)

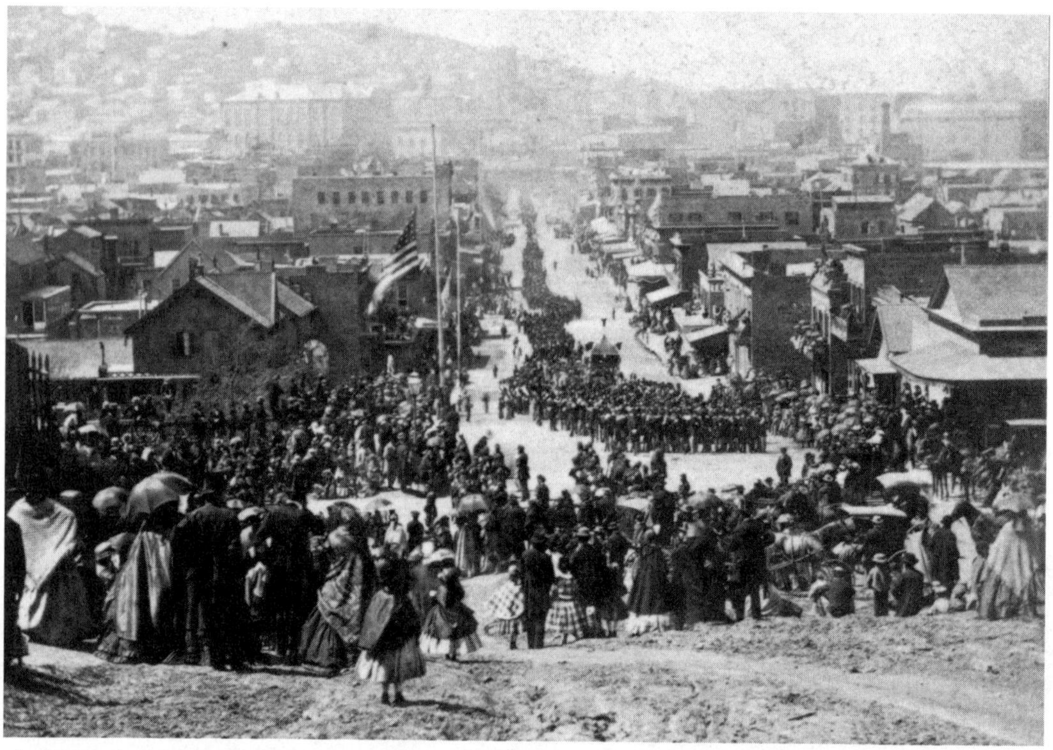

Mock funerals [obsequies] were organized as far west as San Francisco, seen here. This stereoview shows it was a rather ambitious affair. (*Library of Congress*)

General Ulysses S. Grant wears a mourning ribbon in this carte de visite. (*Author's collection*)

There was a tremendous outpouring of grief over President Grant's death in August 1885, twenty years after the Civil War and Grant's acceptance of Lee's surrender. Here America's greatest veteran's funeral procession moves up State Street Hill to the Capitol in Washington. The national funeral rivaled Lincoln's. (*Author's collection*)

Grant's funeral train at Mount McGregor, New York. (*Author's collection*)

President James A. Garfield was given a tremendous farewell in Cleveland in September 1881. Garfield, another Civil War veteran who became president, was the second president to be assassinated. Note the massive funeral arch and catafalque. Lincoln's lavish funeral became the benchmark for future sendoffs. (*Author's collection*)

Surviving his Yankee rival Lincoln by nearly twenty-five years, former Confederate president Jefferson Davis is photographed shortly before his death in 1889. (*Author's collection*)

A portrait of Davis's wife, Varina, taken in 1890. She had spent two years planning her husband's funeral. (*Author's collection*)

The Davis children in an 1867 photograph. From left are Jefferson "Jeff" Jr., Margaret "Maggie," Varina Anne "Winnie," and William "Billy." (*Author's collection*)

Not to be outdone by the North, the South gave Jefferson Davis a flashy farewell. This Louisville & Nashville locomotive headed Davis's funeral train over much of its twelve-hundred-mile journey from New Orleans to Richmond, Virginia, in 1893. He had died in 1889 but was disinterred for a formal funeral and burial.
(*Author's collection*)

At left is a Civil War view of the massive Union Station train shed in Atlanta, Georgia, the one General William Tecumseh Sherman built a special battering ram to demolish. On the right is the replacement shed built during Reconstruction. The Jefferson Davis funeral train stopped here in late May 1893 on its journey from New Orleans to Richmond.
(*Author's collection*)

The funeral car used in the procession for Jefferson Davis in New Orleans. (*Author's collection*)

A view of Jefferson Davis's procession on Royal Street in New Orleans. (*Author's collection*)

The United States was a sensation at the 1904 Saint Louis World's Fair. But an article in the *Saint Louis Republican* newspaper lamented the sad condition of this sacred relic: "Although the car is in a dilapidated condition, plainly showing that it has been abandoned to the cold storms of winter and the sun's hot rays of summer for too many years, it is still the car that was used to bear the remains of President Lincoln from Washington to Springfield, Ill for internment." This view is important because it shows some of the car's furniture. (*Author's collection*)

The shameful stewardship of the United States is evident in this early 1900s image. The four trucks have been replaced with two, no effort has been made to protect the body, and all the paint is worn off, exposing bare wood. The oval that featured the coat of arms is gone from the center of the car. The interior was equally abused, stripped of its elaborate appointments and fitted as a car for workers to camp in until a job was finished. Later it was abandoned to vandals. (*Author's collection*)

In 1866, the Union Pacific Railroad sponsored a highly publicized excursion to the 100th meridian, somewhere along its mainline in Nebraska, using palace cars and the company's newly acquired Lincoln Car, as it came to be called, prominent in this stereoview. Pawnee warriors pose with the excursionists. Along for the ride was Rutherford B. Hayes, who, in ten years, would become the nineteenth president. (*Author's collection*)

The final humiliation: Onlookers linger at the remains of Lincoln's car after it burned in a prairie fire in March 1911. Photo taken by Carl Lewis and made available for this book by his son Richard Lewis.

On May 10, 1865, President Andrew Johnson declared an end to the rebellion and ordered a military procession through the streets of Washington, DC. The Grand Review of the Armies took place May 23–24. Available elements of the Union Army participated in the celebration. Among Johnson's objectives was to lift the country's spirits a month after the assassination. Johnson is seated in the front row of the grandstand, left of center (and to the left of Ulysses S. Grant), observing the review. (*National Archives*)

No matter the cost in money and men, Lincoln was determined he would not be the president who presided over the fracturing of the country. In this Mathew Brady portrait, he bears a forthright, thoughtful gaze. (*Author's collection*)

Robert Lincoln (1843–1926) in a photo taken May 30, 1922, at the dedication of the Lincoln Memorial in Washington. He was the only Lincoln son to reach manhood. Strange historical coincidences found him present at the shootings of two American presidents: James Garfield, in Washington on July 2, 1881, and William McKinley, in Buffalo, New York, on September 6, 1901. As a boy he was saved from serious injury or possible death by Edwin Booth, brother of his father's assassin. Robert was secretary of war from 1881 to 1885, and later became president of the Pullman Palace Car Company. (*Library of Congress*)

Robert Lincoln's children, left to right: Jessie, Mary "Mamie," and Abraham Lincoln II. (*Author's collection*)

Daughters Mary (left) and Jessie as young women. (*Author's collection*)

Jessie Harlan Beckwith Lincoln (1875–1948) was the last surviving descendent to carry Lincoln's surname and was the mother of Robert Todd Lincoln Beckwith, the last surviving descendent of the president. He died in 1985, rendering the family line extinct. Through the triumph and tragedy of that great—and quirky—American family, together with the lessons of courage and self-sacrifice they taught, many of us feel they somehow live on through us. We are incapable of relegating them to the dust of time, least of all Old Abe. (*Author's collection*)

BIBLIOGRAPHY

Books

Alexander, Edwin P. *The Pennsylvania Railroad: A Pictorial History*. New York: Bonanza, 1947.

Burlingame, Michael. *The Inner World of Abraham Lincoln*. Urbana: University of Illinois Press, 1994.

Donald, David Herbert. *Lincoln*. New York: Simon and Schuster, 1996.

Faust, Drew Gilpin. *This Republic of Suffering*. New York: Vintage, 2008.

Schotter, H. W. *The Growth and Development of the Pennsylvania Railroad*. Philadelphia: Allen Books, 1927.

Stevens, Barlow Walter. *A Reporter's Lincoln*. Lincoln: University of Nebraska Press, 1998.

Swanson, James L. *Bloody Crimes: The Funeral of Abraham Lincoln and the Chase for Jefferson Davis*. New York: Harper Perennial, 2010.

Temple, Wayne C. *Abraham Lincoln: From Skeptic to Prophet*. Mahomet, IL: Mayhaven, 1995.

Weissenborn, G. *American Locomotive Engineering*. New York: Glenwood, 1874.

White, John H., Jr. *A History of the American Locomotive: Its Development,1830–1880*. New York: Dover, 1979.

Internet

Abraham Lincoln Birthplace National Historical Park. "Abraham Lincoln's Boyhood Home at Knob Creek." www.nps.gov/abli/Planyourvisit/boyhood-home.htm.

Abraham Lincoln Online. "Lincoln Legal Career Timeline." Accessed March 10, 2015. www.abrahamlincolnonline.org/lincoln/education.lawhighlights.htm.

———. "Mary Lincoln at Bellevue Place." Accessed April 16, 2015. http://www.abrahamlincolnonline.org/lincoln/sites/bellevue.htm.

———. "Pre-Presidential Political Timeline." Accessed March 10, 2015. www.abrahamlincolnonline.org?lincoln/education/polbrief.htm.

———. "White House Funeral Sermon for President Lincoln." Accessed March 10, 2015. www.abrahamlincolnonline.org/lincoln/speeches/gurley.htm.

Abraham Lincoln's Classroom. "The Funeral Train of Abraham Lincoln." Accessed March 10, 2015. abraham lincoln classroom.org?/abraham lincoln in death/the-funeral-train-of-abraham-lincoln/#lft.

Behn, Richard J. "Abraham Lincoln's Beautiful Face." Abraham Lincoln's Classroom. Accessed March 10, 2015. http://abrahamlincolnsclassroom.org/abraham-lincoln-in-depth/abraham-lincolns-beautiful-face-by-richard-j-behn/.

Brooks, Noah. *Washington in Lincoln's Time*. New York: Century, 1896. Accessed April 1, 2015. https://archive.org/details/washingtoninlinc00broo.

Chetwynd, Sally Morong "Sam." "Abraham Lincoln and the Extinction of His Line." February 14, 2011. *Brass Castle Arts* (blog). Accessed March 10, 2015. http://brasscastlearts.blogspot.com/search?qAbraham+Lincoln%3A+His+Ancestry.

Chicago Historical Society. "The Bloody Evidence." Accessed February 14, 2013. http://www/chicagohistory.org/wetwithblood/bloody/coat/coat2.htm.

Coggeshall, William T. *Lincoln Memorial: The Journeys of Abraham Lincoln*. Columbus, OH: Ohio State Journal, 1865. Accessed April 16, 2015. https://books.google.com/books?id=9f_s-CHjYn8C&pg=PA204&lpg=PA204&dq=william+turner+coggeshall,+Lincoln+lincoln+memorial,+new+york+tribune&source=bl&ots=nedoS24MnG&sig=qgcRLzHeO_b_q6EO3fifUkJf554&hl=en&sa=X&ei=9lcwVZ-VEPbbsAT5gYHQDQ&ved=0CB4Q6AEwAA#v=onepage&q=william%20turner%20coggeshall%2C%20Lincoln%20lincoln%20memorial%2C%20new%20york%20tribune&f=false.

Cressey, Pamela. "Twist of Fate Changed Opulent Car into Hearse." May 25,1995. *Historic Alexandria*. Accessed May 27, 2013. http://alexandriava.gov/historic/info/default.aspx?id=41930.

Elliot, Geoff. "Lincoln's Funeral in New York." April 25, 2010. *The Abraham Lincoln Blog*. Accessed January 28, 2013. http://abrahamlincolnblog.blogspot.com/2010/04lincolns-funeral-in-new-york.html.

Goldman, Steve. "The Last Newspaper to Report the Lincoln Assassination." History Buff.com. Accessed January 11, 2013. http://www.historybuff.com/library/reflinclast.html.

Harrell, Carolyn L. *When the Bells Tolled for Lincoln: Southern Reaction to the Assassination*. Macon, GA: Mercer University Press, 1997. Accessed March 10, 2015. webpages.charter.net/lincolnbooks/Harrell.html.

Hart, Dick. "Lincoln's Funeral—May, 1865." February 24, 2007. *Lincoln's Springfield* (blog). Accessed March 10, 2015. http://lincolnsspringfield.blogspot.com/.

Helm, Katherine. *The True Story of Mary, Wife of Lincoln*. Accessed April 13, 2015. https://archive.org/details/truestoryofmaryw00helm.

Key Boards for Christ. "Lincoln's Inaugural Train Journey." Accessed March 10, 2015. keyboardsforchrist.com/Firsttrainride.html.

Kurnhardt III, Philip B. "Lincoln's Contested Legacy." *Smithsonian*, February 1, 2009. Accessed February 2, 2013. http://www.smithsoniamag.com/history-archaeology/ Lincolns-Contested-Legacy-44978351/?no-ist.

Leal, Charles A. *Lincoln's Last Hours*. Accessed March 10, 2015. http://www.gutenberg.org/ebooks/24088?msg=welcome_stranger.

Library of Congress online catalogue. Prints & Photographs Online Catalog. Accessed March 10, 2015. http://www.loc.gov/pictures/search/?q=lincoln%20funeral.

Lincoln Financial Foundation Collection. *The Assassination of Abraham Lincoln.* Accessed April 13, 2015. https://archive.org/details/assassinationofaloclinc.

Lincoln Home National Historic Site. "Reading 4: Springfield Newspaper Account of Abraham Lincoln Funeral." Accessed March 10, 2015. http://www.nps.gov/nr/twhp/wwwlps/lessons/127liho/127facts4.htm.

Lyon, Debbi. "Lincoln Funeral Train in Erie, PA." December 1, 2012. *Old Time Erie* (blog). Accessed March 10, 2015. oldtimeerie,blogspot.com/2012/12/lincoln-funeral-train-in-erie-pa.html.

Mr. Lincoln's White House. "Mr Lincoln & His Observers." Accessed March 10, 2015. www.mrlincolnswhitehouse.org/inside.asp?ID=18subjectID+0.

National Railway Historical Society. Martisco Station Museum. Accessed March 10, 2015. cnynrhs.org/Martisco.html.

Nicolay, John G., and John Hay. *Abraham Lincoln: A History*. Vol. 9. New York: Century, 1890. Accessed April 14, 2015. https://archive.org/details/abrahamlincolna08haygoog.

Open Library: Internet Archives. Jay Monaghan. "An Analysis of Lincoln's Funeral Sermons." Accessed March 10, 2015. https://archive.org/detailsoflincol00mona.

Polce Cruiser. "Lincoln Funeral Train." Railroad.net. Acccessed March 10, 2015. http://www.railroad.net/forums/search.php?keywords=lincoln+funeral+train.

Politics & Politicians. "1,700 Miles of Mourners." Accessed March 10, 2015. civilwarblue-grass.net?PoliticsAndPoliticians/lincolnfuneral.html.

Porter, William S. "The Lincoln Funeral Train." *Illinois State Historical Society Journal* 9. Accessed March 10, 2015. https://archive.org/details/jstor-40194188#page/n1/mode/2up.

Power, J. C. *Abraham Lincoln: His Great Funeral Cortege, from Washington City to Springfield, Illinois, with a History and Description of the National Lincoln Monument*. Springfield: Published by author, 1872. Accessed April 13, 2015. https://archive.org/details/abrahamlincol2383powe.

Railfan. "Buffalo Central Terminal and the Railroad Passenger." Accessed March 10, 2015. central.terminal.railfan.net/history.html.

Schwartz, Barry. "Mourning and the Making of a Sacred Symbol: Durkheim and the Lincoln Assassination." *Social Forces* 70, no. 2 (December 1991). Accessed February 15, 2013. http://www.jstor.org/discover/10.2307/2580243?uid=3739832&uid=2&uid=4&uid=3739256&sid=21106431597853.

Smith, H. Stephen. "Locomotives That Pulled Abraham Lincoln through York County: Lincoln Funeral Train." September 2, 2013. *YorksPast* (blog). Accessed November 29, 2013. http://www/yourkblog.compast/2013/09/02locomtive-that-pulled-abraham-lincoln-through-york-county-lincoln-funeral-train/.

Sweet, W. W. "Bishop Mathew Simpson and the Funeral of Abraham Lincoln." Accessed March 10, 2015. https://archive.org/details/jstor-40193943.

Taylor, Paul. “The Lincoln Hearse Passing Grace Church at 10th and Broadway, N.Y. City, Apr. 25th, 1865 @ approx 3:11 pm.” US National Archives Photostream. Accessed March 10, 2015. https://flickr.com/search/?sort=relevance&text=lincoln%20funeral%9620york%20city.

Wikimedea Commons. “Lincoln’s Funeral on Pennsylvania Ave.” Accessed March 10, 2015. https://commons.wikimedea.org?wiki/File:Lincoln’s_funeral_on_Pennsylvania_Ave_(LOC)_325291551).jpg.

Wikipedia. “Assassination of Abraham Lincoln.” Accessed March 10, 2015. https//en.wikipedia.org/wiki.Assassination_of_Abraham Lincoln.

———. “List of Photographs of Abraham Lincoln” Accessed March 10, 2015. https://en.wikipedia.org/wiki/List_of_photographs_of_Abraham_Lincoln.

Wilentz, Sean. *The Best American History Essays on Lincoln*. Accessed March 10, 2015. https://books.google.com/books?id=66GKsgHO-pwC&pg=PA256&lpg=PA256&dq=the+best+american+history+essays+on+lincoln&source=bl&ots=ni1X-MmDyu&sig=SxHKztoyhbKd_oj3ac6XHihVSyY&hl=en&sa=X&ei=1KQqVfyUJ4eqgwS9sIHoDw&ved=0CEkQ6AEwBg#v=onepage&q=the%20best%20american%20history%20essays%20on%20lincoln&f=false.